KEEP LOOKING UP

Books by Jentezen Franklin

Love Like You've Never Been Hurt
Restart Your Heart
Acres of Diamonds
Overcoming When You Feel Overwhelmed

KEEP LOOKING UP

40 DAYS TO BUILDING YOUR TRUST IN GOD

JENTEZEN FRANKLIN

Chosen

a division of Baker Publishing Group

Minneapolis, Minnesota

© 2023 by Jentezen Franklin

Published by Chosen Books
Minneapolis, Minnesota
www.chosenbooks.com

Chosen Books is a division of
Baker Publishing Group, Grand Rapids, Michigan

Printed in the United States of America

Library of Congress Cataloging-in-Publication Data
Names: Franklin, Jentezen, 1962- author. | Franklin, Jentezen, 1962– Overcoming when you feel overwhelmed.
Title: Keep looking up : 40 days to building your trust in God / Jentezen Franklin.
Description: Minneapolis, Minnesota : Chosen Books, a division of Baker Publishing Group, [2023] | Includes bibliographical references.
Identifiers: LCCN 2022060975 | ISBN 9780800762919 (cloth) | ISBN 9781493439386 (ebook)
Subjects: LCSH: Spiritual formation—Devotional calenders. | Anxiety—Religious aspects—Christianity. | Conflict management—Religious aspects—Christianity.
Classification: LCC BV4511 .F724 2023 | DDC 248.4—dc23/eng/20230329
LC record available at https://lccn.loc.gov/2022060975

Cover design by LOOK Design Studio

Author represented by The Fedd Agency, Inc.

Baker Publishing Group publications use paper produced from sustainable forestry practices and post-consumer waste whenever possible.

23   24   25   26   27   28   29   7   6   5   4   3   2   1

CONTENTS

INTRODUCTION

A nest is a safe place. It evokes feelings of security and comfort. It's homey. But God doesn't intend for us to get so comfortable in our nests that we don't want to leave. Even mother birds must ruffle their nests to get their young to fly on their own. God will do the same for you and me. When we get too comfortable, too content, too complacent, God will allow our nests to be busted up so we can learn how to fly.

Does it feel like your nest is being busted up? Are you overwhelmed? I know what that feels like. I've been in the place where I knew God was taking me because of what He promised in His Word, yet at the same time I didn't understand why certain things were happening.

We were not born to live and die in our nests. We are destined for higher ground. The enemy knows you have a heavenly calling and are pregnant with the promises of God. That's why the attacks are plenty. Think of it this way: Jacob had to be crippled before he was crowned with a new name, Israel. Joseph had to go through the pit to get to the palace.

Remember Job, the man in the Bible who lost almost everything? He cried out, "I shall die in my nest." In the most tragic of circumstances, Job had to face some tough questions. Sooner or later, we must face the same ones:

1. **Can God be trusted when I suffer**? Job lost his family, his finances, his physical health, even his reputation. But amid the unimaginable losses and heartbreak, he learned how to praise God like never before. Yes, Job could trust God in his grief and pain.

2. **Can God be trusted when people I love forsake me?** Job wrote, "My relatives have failed, and my close friends have forgotten me" (Job 19:14). If you've been abandoned, rejected or forsaken by ones you've loved the most, be encouraged. Like Job, you must see that there is One who will never leave or forsake you. Yes, Job could trust God when his friends and family weren't there for him.

3. **Can God be trusted when I walk through extreme darkness?** Job was in absolute darkness. Are you there right now? Job thought God owed him some answers, but God never answered his questions. Can you trust God when He gives you no explanations and no light? God eventually did remind Job of His sovereignty, sufficiency and sympathy. Job responded with praise, and God restored Job double. Yes, Job could trust God in the midst of darkness.

I love what Job said, "Though He slay me, yet will I trust Him" (Job 13:15). I hope and pray that you can say the same thing. And through these pages, I want to remind and keep reminding you that God can be trusted in your overwhelming times.

This is especially important to take to heart because we are living in the last days. Jesus is coming back one day soon. Luke 18:8 asks, "Nevertheless, when the Son of Man comes, will He really find faith on the earth?" What a telling question! It doesn't take much faith to sit around and moan and groan in a busted nest. Faith demands the use of our wings. I don't know about you, but I'd rather fail at trying to fly than sit in the nest, waiting to die.

We need to live as if we believe that Jesus Christ could come at any minute. We need to live as if we have overcome, and to do this, we must learn how to endure through the hard times.

This 40-day devotional is based on what I call 5 Steps to Overcoming through Overwhelming Times. These steps are anchored in the words of Jesus and the conversation He shared with His disciples while they were at Herod's temple (see Matthew 24). Jesus' followers asked Him for signs of the last days, and instead of providing them with the answers they wanted, His message was meant to prepare His followers spiritually, emotionally and mentally for what was to come.

These 5 Steps will help you be courageous and full of hope as you endure the race of faith and ensuing chaos of every day that lies before you.

- Step #1 Look Within
- Step #2 Look to Jesus
- Step #3 Look Ahead
- Step #4 Look Out
- Step #5 Look Up

As you work through these steps, I encourage you to keep a journal nearby to record your thoughts and responses to the prompts.

You may feel like your nest is busted, like you're tumbling and falling and absolutely overwhelmed, but know that because you have a Father in heaven who can fly faster than you can fall, you are overcoming!

LOOK WITHIN

Global health crises. Political turmoil. Social divisions. Environmental calamities. Wars, and more wars. We live in days like none before. The signs of Jesus' return are everywhere you look. It's both exciting and terrifying.

When the disciples peppered Jesus with questions about the end times, though Jesus did offer some idea of what the end would look like, His first response for His disciples then and for us today was to "take heed" or "look within" (see Matthew 24:4).

Prophecies are not intended for our speculation; they are for our motivation. Instead of being concerned about the signs of the times, Jesus wants us to take spiritual inventory . . . to check ourselves, first and foremost. His return is motivation for us to get on our knees, to get our families right, to watch our temptations, to determine if we're truly serving God or settling for a lukewarm faith. My prayer is for the devotionals in the first part of this book to help show you how.

Watch Your Words

Death and life are in the power of the tongue,
And those who love it will eat its fruit.

Proverbs 18:21

Jesus gave us great advice found in Mark 13:33: "Take heed, watch and pray; for you do not know when the time is." Take note of the word *watch*. In the next few days, I'll share with you five aspects of your life that you need to *W.A.T.C.H.* in order to overcome:

W — your Words
A — your Attitude
T — your Temptations
C — your Character
H — your Household

What is your overall outlook on life? Are you an optimist or a pessimist? Do you tend to see silver linings, or do you mostly see gray skies and rain? Think about this: God spoke the world into creation, then He created man in His image . . . and gave him the power to speak! What does that mean for you and me? God says in Isaiah 57:19 that He creates the fruit of our lips. The words we say affect our world.

Words change the atmosphere of your life. You can speak life or you can speak death. You can speak depression or you can speak joy. You can speak hopelessness or you can speak faith. It's up to you! I want to give three sources for your words so you can watch with better diligence what comes out of your mouth.

1. Watch the words that come your way from the devil. When Jesus predicted His death and resurrection as recorded in Matthew 16, Peter took Jesus aside and rebuked Him. Jesus' response? "Get thee behind me, Satan" (Matthew 16:23 KJV). Peter was saying things that were not of God, and God needed to check those words. If you are chained to an addiction, grieving the loss of a loved one or struggling under a pile of debt, the devil is going to tell you to quit, that you won't make it and that you'll always be a failure. Recognize the words of the enemy, and rebuke them with a word from the Lord that you are loved, saved, delivered and healed.

2. Watch the words that come from other people. Have you ever had a great day and suddenly you hear or see one negative comment from someone, and it ruins everything? This happens to the best of us—but it doesn't have to affect us so deeply. Don't turn your ears into garbage cans. Be selective with what you receive from other people. Leave the words from others that speak inferiority, defeat or negativity alone. Don't allow that kind of language to dampen your overcoming spirit.

3. Watch your own words. We are to speak words of life. We are to speak words of faith. We are to speak words that agree with God. We are to speak what God speaks over ourselves, our families and our communities.

Never speak words that allow the enemy to think he's winning. If you're going to be an overcomer, you're going to have to watch your words. Send your words in the direction you want them to go.

PRAY

Lord, You know every part of me—who I am, the thoughts that live in my deepest places, every word I've ever heard and spoken . . . everything I've ever done. Teach me to discern all of these, to stop each word and each thought at the door of my mind and identify its source. Then, give me both wisdom and strength to receive only those that come from You. I want my decisions and my actions to glorify You, and to be an overcomer. In Jesus' name, I pray. Amen.

REFLECT

Words are like seeds. Just as your garden produces plants based on the seeds you sow, so it is with the words you speak over your life, your future and your family. How have you seen words give life or create death?

ACT

For the next seven days, challenge yourself to take a fast from negative words. You are not allowed to complain about the temperature outside, your nosy neighbor, the President of the United States, how your body looks, how loud the music was in church . . . you get the idea. Take note of when you consider saying something negative, or when you begin to utter a negative statement. How hard is it for you to stop the habit? When the fast is over, look over your notes. Consider being more intentional about what you say.

Watch Your Attitude

You must have the same attitude that Christ Jesus had.

Philippians 2:5 NLT

How many jobs are lost every day because of employees' negative outlooks? How many people are passed over for a promotion because they approach their work and the people around them with complaints or hostility? How many marriages fall apart because of a lack of gratitude? It would be impossible to calculate. No one should ever lose a job, miss a promotion, or destroy a marriage because of a poor attitude. Why? Because a person's attitude is not set; it is a choice.

I have learned through experience that a person's attitude can tell me a lot about their level of faith. People with great faith approach situations differently because they know the battle is won before they ever enter the room. They take the high road because they know it's not all about them. Having a good attitude not only speaks volumes of a person's faith walk, but also says something about their physical well-being.

According to a Johns Hopkins study, people with a family history of heart disease and a good attitude were one-third less likely to have a heart attack or other heart event within five to twenty-five years compared to those with a more negative attitude.[1] Medical doctors and scientists don't exactly know what to call it, but there is a clear connection between having a positive outlook and protection from the inflammatory damage of stress.[2]

It's not easy to have a good attitude all the time. At times, in fact, it's near impossible. Yet, the Bible tells us to mirror the kind of attitude that Christ Jesus had when He walked on this earth. He always approached people with love, grace, acceptance and a heart to serve rather than be served.

The ancient King David asked God to "renew a right spirit within me" (Psalm 51:10 ESV). Even when, or rather especially when, we're in a spiritually dry season or life feels overwhelming, we need to remain steadfast in the attitude that God is still good, He is still faithful, He still loves us and He will never leave us.

While we don't know what tomorrow will bring or how God will answer our prayer, in every situation we encounter there is always one thing we have complete control over: our attitude. Our attitude determines our approach to a situation. We can escalate or manage it; bring tension to it or speak calm over it; rest in faith in it or toil in anxiety because of it. If you truly believe that the Lord works all things together for your good, then start there. Start knowing that God is going to bring something good into your situation—that He has your best interests in mind. Decide your attitude and God will take care of the rest.

— PRAY —

Father, bless and keep us today, and give us the spirit that says, "God, I'm grateful." If all You ever did for me was to send Your Son to die for me, it would have been more than enough. Forgive me for the times I lose sight of that and instead develop a complaining and griping attitude. Develop in me an attitude of gratitude that cannot be shaken. Today, I will give thanks, for You are good and Your love endures forever. In Jesus' name, I pray. Amen.

— REFLECT —

If the Bible says we're supposed to have an attitude like Jesus, what are three things you should be doing today to imitate His behavior and actions?

— ACT —

At the end of Day 1, we learned to discern our thoughts and allow only those that are from God to enter the door of our minds. Now, when we identify thoughts that aren't His, instead of throwing them out, let's immediately replace them with thoughts that we know come from Him.

Watch Your Temptations

Therefore submit to God. Resist the devil and he will flee from you.

James 4:7

If you're going to watch your life, you must watch your temptations. All of us get tempted. No one is exempt.

Have you ever felt guilty when you feel an urge to click on a particular website, or linger a little longer where you know you shouldn't, or pick up whatever destructive habit is numbing your anxiety? Sometimes we get discouraged and think, "If I were a better Christian, I wouldn't have such thoughts. I've prayed over and over. *Why doesn't God just take this temptation away?*"

Here's a secret that's not so secret: Temptation never goes away. Good news is that God will give you power over it.

When the Israelites entered the Promised Land, they thought they were done with temptation, with lack, with conflict. They were surprised that the Canaanites were still in the land. Thinking they must have gone the wrong way, they got discouraged. "Surely this couldn't be the land of promise." Yet, God's Word makes it clear that the Christian life, from start to finish, is warfare. Paul says we are called to "wrestle . . . against principalities, against powers, against the rulers of the darkness of this world, against spiritual wickedness in high places" (Ephesians 6:12 KJV).

Just like the Promised Land, the promised life of victory requires you to deal with temptation and wrestle your way through to victory, believing that "greater is he that is in you, than he that is in the world" (1 John 4:4 KJV). Indeed, their enemy's attack proved that Israel was in the Promised Land. So experiencing temptations is proof you are truly abiding in Christ.

Note that temptation isn't sin. The sin only occurs when you yield to it. The enemy will try hard to get you to blame yourself for the temptations you experience. Why? Because when you believe that you are the source of it, you feel condemned and discouraged. As you indulge in feelings of discouragement, you become easy prey and Satan convinces you to go ahead and yield to the temptation. Ironically, you yield to sin through the fear of having already fallen.

The Bible says that Jesus can sympathize with our weaknesses because He was tempted in all the same ways we are, yet He didn't fall into sin (see Hebrews 4:15). He was aware of the emotional roller coaster some of us experience. He knew what it was like to be tempted. There is no greater example from whom we can learn than Jesus.

So when you are tempted—when you stare at the phone and feel the urge to text someone you shouldn't, or pour yourself another drink or rack up another credit card bill—know you have a choice. You can yield to it or say no.

Practice resisting the enemy's attacks to get you to do things you know are wrong. When you're tempted, reject Satan's condemnation and reach for Christ's overcoming assistance.

— PRAY —

God, the battle against temptation is so strong. Sometimes I feel too weak to fight it. I pray for Your strength to overwhelm me and give me the power to walk away when the enemy tries to entice me. Forgive me for anything that is not pleasing to You. Help me to stay pure and focused on You. And thank You for the example of Jesus Christ on earth who had the power to overcome the devil's temptations. I am so grateful that power is the same power that lives within me. In Jesus' name, I pray. Amen.

— REFLECT —

When are you most vulnerable to temptation? How can you better care for that area of weakness so you are more likely to say no than to indulge in the temptation?

— ACT —

In the reflection above, you should have identified some area of weakness in your own life. This isn't anything to feel guilty about; we all have weaknesses. After acknowledging yours, identify what God's Word says about that issue . . . how He calls us to think, believe and behave in that area. Then, make the commitment to choose God's way over your own. When the temptation returns, immediately focus on Him, His way, and don't look (or think) in any other direction. The more you take His way over yours, the more you'll see and reap the benefits, and the easier it'll become to say no to the enemy and yes to Him.

Watch Your Character

Whoever walks in integrity walks securely, but he who makes his ways crooked will be found out.

Proverbs 10:9 ESV

Bobby Jones is arguably one of the best golfers in history that you've probably never heard of. He is the only golfer to have achieved the grand slam of golf—winning all four of golf's professional tournaments in one calendar year. Jones never turned pro. He remained an amateur golfer his entire career.

Jones was known not only for his golfing talent but also for his integrity. During the 1925 U.S. Open, Jones unintentionally caused his golf ball to move. It was a one-stroke penalty. No one saw it, so technically no one could call him out on it. Still, Jones didn't need an onlooker to tell him what he needed to do. He called a foul on himself. The honest move cost him the win, and he lost the game by one stroke. While Jones was praised for his act of integrity, his response was, "There is only one way to play the game. You might as well praise a man for not robbing a bank."[3] Jones could have won the game, but he would have lost his integrity in the process. In doing the right thing, this man also protected the honor of the game.

Character matters. God is not as interested in your talent, your bank account, or how many Bible verses you post on social media as He is in your character. Overcomers understand the importance of good character. It's not about what we look like when everyone is watching; it's about who we are when no one is looking.

If you're going to overcome fear, depression, anxiety and addiction, you have to be the same in the dark as you are in the light. Like David, you must defeat your inner lion and bear before you can go out and defeat Goliath in public. If you can win in the dark of your life, behind closed doors, it'll only be a matter of time before great victory will manifest in the open where everyone will see it. This is your character.

There must be a call to character if you're going to overcome in a world that overwhelms. Be the same in the dark as you are in the light, be the same at home as you are at work, let your character speak for you, and fight the good fight when no one is looking. Then, when everyone *is* looking, you'll be positioned to win!

Watch your character. Keep your word. Take care of your responsibilities. If you say you're going to do something, do it. If you put up a particular image in public, make sure it matches the one you have in private.

── PRAY ──

Heavenly Father, I confess before You the times I have failed and fallen short of Your glory. Help me to walk in spirit and in truth each day, conformed to Your spirit, not to what society or culture dictates. I want to be a person of integrity. I want to live in a way that is pleasing before You. Help me to do that. Thank You for being faithful to me when I wasn't faithful to You. In Jesus' name, I pray. Amen.

── REFLECT ──

What does your social media feed look like? What does it say about your character?

── ACT ──

To meet the challenge of making decisions with a healthy balance of what others think of you and the value you hold for the things you want, write a mission statement for your life. What roles does your life fulfill, and how do you feel that God has called you to carry them out? Write it down. Then, as opportunities and decisions come up in your life, weigh those thoughts and decisions against your mission statement before taking action.

Watch Your Household

For I have chosen him, that he may command his children and his household after him to keep the way of the Lord by doing righteousness and justice, so that the Lord may bring to Abraham what he has promised him.

Genesis 18:19 ESV

The Bible tells us that Abraham's nephew, Lot, was once kidnapped. Lot's father, Abraham's brother, died so Abraham took Lot in as his own son. When Lot was captured by five enemy armies, Abraham knew that if he tried to coordinate a rescue attempt, he would be far outnumbered. But he did it anyway. Abraham was willing to pay any price to get his nephew back—and with God's grace, his plan worked.

Abraham believed in, invested in and fought for his family. I don't know the dynamics of your family, but I know the importance of watching your household. Don't be a bystander. Be committed to being present and intentional in leading and serving the ones you love.

I want to give you five ways to be a watchful guide in your family and help them succeed.

1. **Openly communicate with and express love to your loved ones.** God knows that as parents we make mistakes. But we cannot do things that will mess our kids up if our kids know that their mom and dad love each other and are committed to one another. Kids also need our parental affirmation. If they do not get affirmation from you, they are going to get it from someone else!

2. **Establish, communicate and enforce boundaries.** We need to teach our children what boundaries are. What is the standard in your home? What are your boundaries? What rules have you set in place for your children and even for yourself? Set the stage for what will and will not be tolerated. And be sure both you and your spouse are on the same page.

3. **Be committed to the process.** Just because one of your kids, say, your son, is freaking out and messing up right now, know he is not going to be like that the rest of his life. Be patient and let the Lord complete His work in him.

4. **Place Jesus above all else.** Invite the presence of Jesus into your home at all times . . . even in the little things. Acknowledge Him in every meal, through grateful attitudes, through reading the Bible together and praying as a family.

5. **Lead by example**. We teach through what our kids see us do in real life. My kids learn about forgiveness when they see me mess up and ask for forgiveness. Do not just preach to them; live out what you say.

Don't become so preoccupied with schedules and routines, and so overwhelmed with responsibilities—I know there are many!—that your priority to love and serve your family gets left behind. Watch what goes on in your household!

PRAY

Dear Lord, I haven't always led my family in the way that is right before You. Forgive me for not having a watchful eye under my own roof. Help me to commit to seeing our family succeed and follow You. I want to be an example for my loved ones. I pray for Your blessing and protection over our household. Be gracious toward us. Show us Your favor and give us Your peace. In Jesus' name, I pray. Amen.

REFLECT

What habits have you established in your family that foster God's guidance and leading of a spiritual home and lifestyle?

— ACT —

Plan a date night with your spouse to discuss and decide on three of the most important values you want to establish within your family together. Talk about how you will implement these into your family life, write them down, then find a way to share them with your children during a family night. Values lead to actions, and repeated actions lead to habits.

View Offenses as Opportunities

It is impossible that no offenses should come.

Luke 17:1

There's a story told about Muhammad Ali, former heavy-weight boxing champion and one of the most famous sports figures of the twentieth century. He was on a plane, and the flight attendant noticed that he hadn't put his seat-belt on. Firmly but kindly, she asked him to please fasten his seatbelt. Ali refused despite the flight attendant's persistent demands. Finally, the boxing champion exclaimed, "Super-man don't need no seatbelt." The flight attendant's response? "And Superman don't need no airplane, either."

No one is Superman. No one is Wonder Woman. We all have vulnerabilities and weaknesses. We're all susceptible to being hurt and offended. In fact, Jesus told His disciples in Luke 17:1, "It is impossible that no offenses should come."

One way or another, we are all going to get offended, hurt, insulted, betrayed, cheated, shamed, violated or lose our pride.

Since offenses are a reality of which we are warned about in the Bible, we may need to think of them through a different lens. Take, for example, the following suggestion: Did you know that airplanes take off into a headwind? The resistance gives them lift and gets them off the ground quickly. I want you to think of offenses as opposition that functions the same way. None of us wants to be hurt or betrayed, but sometimes the bad things that happen to us can bring some good.

In Day 3, I talked about how we should all strive to emulate the life of Jesus. Just think of the number of times He could have been offended. He was criticized continually. His enemies called Him a drunk and a glutton (see Matthew 11:19). He was accused of being possessed by a demon (see John 8:48). He was even betrayed by those closest to Him. Yet Jesus never allowed bitterness or discouragement to defeat Him. He used offenses to demonstrate grace, to heal, to love, to forgive.

Though the enemy might intend for the wounds of life to destroy you, your soul, your worship, your joy, your dream, your marriage and your family, God has a different plan. Isaiah 53:5 tells us that Jesus was wounded for our transgressions. Take note of two key words in that statement: He was *wounded* for our *transgressions*. Could it be that the offenses you are dealing with are an opportunity to help someone else down the road? Could it be that the hell you are going through today will heal someone else tomorrow?

When someone spreads a rumor about you, betrays your confidence, or breaks your heart, remind yourself that God is good. He can use what looks like your greatest opposition and turn it into your greatest opportunity.

— PRAY —

Lord, sometimes the difficulties and the busyness of life limit my ability to work through and process the offenses I have. Help me to slow down enough and see through Your heart, Your eyes and Your ears so I don't become hardened and stay stuck. I want to minimize my offenses and give myself the ability to see You work the bad things in my life for my good and Your glory. In Jesus' name, I pray. Amen.

— REFLECT —

Think about the last time you turned an offense into an opportunity. What was the outcome? How does this motivate you to do this again and again?

— ACT —

Need some help overcoming offenses? Here are some tips that will help get you there:

1. **Don't seek vengeance**. God will avenge you. "Beloved, do not avenge yourselves . . . for it is written, 'Vengeance is Mine, I will repay,' says the Lord" (Romans 12:19).

2. **Don't be ruled by anger**. "Let every person be quick to hear, slow to speak, slow to anger; for the anger of man does not produce the righteousness of God" (James 1:19–20 ESV).

3. **Forgive those who have offended you**. It's not about keeping score. It's about losing count. "Then Peter came to Him and said, "Lord, how often shall my brother sin against me, and I forgive him? Up to seven times?" Jesus said to him, "I do not say to you, up to seven times, but up to seventy times seven" (Matthew 18:21–22).

4. **Don't give up.** Jesus said, "In the world you will have tribulation; but be of good cheer, I have overcome the world" (John 16:33). Never forget the Overcomer who is in you.

It Is Unforgiveable Not to Forgive

For if you forgive men their trespasses, your heavenly Father will also forgive you. But if you do not forgive men their trespasses, neither will your Father forgive your trespasses.

Matthew 6:14–15

Matthew 18 records a parable Jesus told to His disciples when Peter asked Him questions about forgiveness.

There was a servant who owed his master ten thousand talents. According to scholars, a talent at that time was the equivalent of a thousand dollars today, making the debt a total of about ten million dollars! The servant begged the king for mercy. Moved with compassion, the king agreed to forgive the debt and let the servant go. Just as the highest authority in the kingdom forgave a servant, so Jesus, through the cross, forgives our debt. But that's not the end of the story.

The same servant who just had his debt forgiven came across a fellow servant who owed him some money. Instead of showing this guy the same level of mercy he had just experienced, the first servant took the man by the throat, demanded his money be returned immediately and ultimately threw him in jail for the outstanding debt. The king heard what happened and was appalled. He called the first servant back to his palace and said, "You wicked servant! I forgave you all that debt because you begged me. Should you not also have had compassion on your fellow servant, just as I had pity on you?" (Matthew 18:32–33). The king was so angry, he rescinded his offer of mercy and threw the wicked servant in jail.

It should grip our hearts to know that God has forgiven us of so much, yet we often hold on to the petty offenses from those we call friends. We may never forget the pain caused by others, but we can forgive and move on. The grudge we hold on to causes us more pain than the person who hurt us.

Most importantly, Jesus said it is unforgivable not to forgive. If you refuse to forgive others, God will not forgive you. Do you need God to forgive you for something? If you look within, because you're human, of course you do! I do, too! We are human beings with a sinful nature and in need of a Savior.

Forgive those who have wronged you, betrayed you, cursed you, abused you, harmed you, abandoned you, stolen from you or were unfaithful to you. All of us carry debts we cannot pay. Just as we are forgiven by God through Christ Jesus, we must extend that same grace to others.

— PRAY —

Lord, thank You for dying on the cross for me and coming back to life so I could live a full life on earth and forever with You in eternity. Forgive me when I don't forgive others. Remove from me the burden of bitterness. Soften my heart and my spirit to love others the way You do. Help me to forgive those who hurt me, especially when forgiveness doesn't come naturally or easily. In Jesus' name, I pray. Amen.

— REFLECT —

How well do you forgive others and let things go?

— ACT —

Read Psalm 139:23–24 (NLT): "Search me, O God, and know my heart; test me and know my anxious thoughts. Point out anything in me that offends you, and lead me along the path of everlasting life." Spend time in prayer and ask God to show you if there is unforgiveness in your heart. Now is the time to forgive.

Tell God what happened. Tell Him how it made you feel. Then, ask God to forgive you of bitterness or resentment. Ask Him to forgive you for holding on to the weight of unforgiveness for so long. Then, release forgiveness to the person who has hurt you. Sometimes this is appropriate to do in person, and other times it's okay to do in your heart. Consider meeting with a licensed therapist if the process of forgiveness has uncovered long-held unhealed wounds in your life.

Start Losing Count

Put on tender mercies, kindness, humility, meekness, long-suffering; bearing with one another, and forgiving one another, if anyone has a complaint against another; even as Christ forgave you, so you also must do.

Colossians 3:12-13

I've struggled with math since I was a kid. I have never been good at it. Even today, if I'm paying for a meal at a restaurant and the tip is not included with the bill, whoever I am with had better go ahead and order dessert and coffee because they'll have to wait a while. The Bible can be a great math tutor when it comes to how many times you are to forgive. It tells us exactly what to do with that math when it comes to loving and forgiving people who have hurt us.

Peter asked Jesus, "Lord, how often shall my brother sin against me, and I forgive him? Up to seven times?" (Matthew 18:21). No doubt, Peter was dealing with a difficult person who was truly trying his patience—perhaps a nagging wife, a meddling neighbor or a dishonest fishing partner. We see in Scripture that Peter was a very impatient man with a short temper. Extending forgiveness six times was a big deal for a man of his temperament. I bet, in his mind, seven times was *really* generous. Not according to Jesus.

"I do not say to you, up to seven times, but up to seventy times seven," Jesus replied (see Matthew 18:22). In other words, forgive, then forgive again. And again. And again. And again.

Many of us have trouble forgiving. Instead of releasing offenses, we cling to them for dear life. We add up words and actions that were said to us years ago. We compile hurts, and we hold these hurts forever in our minds. We turn them into mathematical absolutes. And, in the process, we invite unforgiveness into our hearts. It sits. It festers. Often, like a tumor, it grows.

Jesus told us that if we are to be a forgiving people, we can't keep score. We must lose count. If you were to forgive somebody 490 times in a day, that would be an offense every two minutes that must be forgiven. It's continual.

Forgiveness is powerful. It unleashes the Spirit of God. It is the key that will unlock the doors of heaven and usher in peace, blessing and joy. Jesus said, "Whatever you bind on earth will be bound in heaven, and whatever you loose on earth will be loosed in heaven" (Matthew 18:18). You can split hell wide open by releasing forgiveness.

Overcomers forgive. Start today not by keeping score but by losing count.

— PRAY —

Heavenly Father, thank You for dying on the cross for me and for forgiving me of all my sins. Remind me each and every day of Your continual grace and mercy so I can live in a spirit of forgiveness, whether I feel like it or not. Teach me to forget to do math when it comes to forgiving. Help me to know well the peace and the freedom that come with forgiveness so that I might forgive again and again. In Jesus' name, I pray. Amen.

— REFLECT —

How much has God forgiven you in your life?

— ACT —

Think about two ways in which you can develop a lifestyle of forgiving (i.e., changing your attitude or reminding yourself daily of Scripture truths). Then, do them!

LOOK TO JESUS

When storms brew, the key is not to feast your eyes on the raging winds or the driving wind; it is to fix your eyes on Jesus. Jesus told us in Matthew 24:6, "See that you are not troubled." It is not time to panic or crawl under a rock hoping Jesus returns tomorrow. Your job right now is to keep looking to Jesus, the author and finisher of our faith.

A Remedy for Discouragement

Look, the LORD your God has set the land before you; go up and possess it, as the LORD God of your fathers has spoken to you; do not fear or be discouraged.

Deuteronomy 1:21

In the opening scene of the Christmas classic *It's a Wonderful Life*, we are introduced to the main character, George Bailey, by name as a bunch of his friends and family send prayers up to heaven for him. These prayers catch the attention of two angels named Joseph and Franklin, and they decide to send a novice angel, Clarence, down to earth to help George Bailey. Through the conversation with the angels, we learn that George Bailey isn't sick but, according to Joseph, it's much worse. "He's discouraged. At exactly 10:45 p.m. Earth time, that man will be thinking seriously of throwing away God's greatest gift."[1]

Because you're never really defeated until you're defeated on the inside, the devil knows that the greatest thing he can use against the believer is discouragement.

Don't be embarrassed or ashamed if you feel discouraged. Discouragement hits the best of us. John the Baptist reached a point when he was devastated, not only because he had just been thrown into prison, but also because he wanted Jesus to assure him that he was doing the right thing.

Even though it is a natural response that we all face from time to time, there is great danger in allowing this feeling to set up camp in our minds. The moment we become discouraged, we're faced with the tough choice of what to do. Discouragement makes us want to quit, turn back, give up and immediately question all the choices we've made to get to where we are. It's okay to feel discouraged; how you respond to discouragement is up to you.

In Numbers 21:3, the Bible records the defeat of the Canaanites by the Israelites. God had intervened and delivered the enemy into their hands. Yet, in the following verse we see that God's people were loathing their journey to the Promised Land:

> Then they journeyed from Mount Hor by the Way of the Red Sea, to go around the land of Edom; and the soul of the people became very discouraged on the way.
>
> Verse 4

Their complaining forced God to send angry snakes their way that bit them.

When the people humbled themselves and asked God for forgiveness, He gave Moses the remedy for discouragement. God told Moses to make a serpent of brass, put it on a pole and lift it up, and all those who had been bitten would be healed when they looked upon it.

Today, we know exactly whom God sent for us to gaze upon. No matter what you're facing, you must look up. You must look to Jesus to pull you through. Instead of getting shook up, we must get to the place where we look up. Let this be your first response when you feel discouragement creeping in.

PRAY

Lord, some days seem like such a struggle. I believe in You and I love You, but these challenges have me feeling down. Please give me the strength to get through this and the wisdom to know what to do. In the midst of the storm, may my eyes be fixed on You. Thank You for being my rock and my fortress. You are worthy of all the praise. In Jesus' name, I pray. Amen.

REFLECT

It takes courage to admit one is discouraged. Many people find it hard to admit discouragement to others. Why should believers not be afraid to admit their struggle in this?

⸺ ACT ⸺

One of the best ways to look to Jesus when discouragement sets in is to praise and worship Him. Put on some music and soak in His presence. Let praise be your strategy. You could be one "hallelujah" away from your breakthrough.

Stay Focused

Let your eyes look straight ahead,
And your eyelids look right before you.
Ponder the path of your feet,
And let all your ways be established.
Do not turn to the right or the left;
Remove your foot from evil.

Proverbs 4:25–27

Tino Wallenda is the sixth generation of wire walkers—high-wire circus performers who do not use safety nets—in the Wallenda family. Known as The Flying Wallendas, his family is named in the Guinness Book of World Records for their high-wire eight-person pyramid. Tino has performed some impressive feats. He's walked the wire between high-rise buildings, the tallest being the Denver D&F Tower, a reach of 189 feet into the air. He walked to the tower from a crane that was set 3,300 feet away. He has also walked the wire over rivers, over waterfalls, over tigers and once over a swimming pool filled with more than fifty man-eating sharks.

Tino's grandfather, Karl Wallenda, who crossed Tallulah Falls Gorge and performed two headstands in the middle of that walk, taught Tino how to maintain balance on the wire. Read what Tino says of his grandfather:

> The most important thing he ever taught me was to put my focus on an un-moving point at the far end of the wire and never let my attention waver. Over and over again, he drilled into my thick skull the importance of maintaining my balance by focusing on this fixed point. That lesson has saved me from disaster on the tightrope so many times in my career—but it has also helped me in my day-to-day life.[2]

The minute life gets overwhelming, we tend to stop looking at Jesus and focus on the problem instead. The enemy loves when we do that. Distraction is one of his favorite strategies. Satan doesn't want you to fix your eyes on Jesus; he wants to distract you from Him.

When Jesus was in the wilderness fasting for forty days, Satan offered distractions to try to draw Him away from God's purpose. The devil came to Him and told Him there was an easier way. He didn't have to spend all that time praying. "I'll give you everything you want," Satan told Jesus, "if you'll just bow down and worship me" (see Matthew 4:3).

What was Jesus' response? He said, "It is written, 'Man shall not live by bread alone, but by every word that proceeds out of the mouth of God'" (Matthew 4:4). Even Jesus wasn't immune to the distractions of this world. Yet, in His case, contrary to what the devil tried to tempt Him with, He chose to remain focused on the truth that bread and material things are not to be the sole purpose of life.

What is distracting you away today from focusing on Jesus, on the Word of God, on prayer and on believing the promises of God rather than worrying about your job (or lack thereof), your child's behavior at school or the addiction that eats away at your false sense of control?

Stop letting your focus move in the wind's every direction. Look to Jesus!

— PRAY —

God in heaven, it's been hard to avoid allowing the distractions of life to take over my focus. The rote distractions and the challenges I encounter that seem too much to handle distract me from looking to You. Settle my spirit and center my soul on You. You are the Bread of Life, my Sustenance, my Provider, my Healer and the One who delivers me. Thank You for always being there for me. In Jesus' name, I pray. Amen.

— REFLECT —

What are two things that are destabilizing your gaze from remaining fixed on Jesus?

— ACT —

Think about your answer to the question above. Now, read Philippians 3:13–14:

> I do not count myself to have apprehended; but one thing I do, forgetting those things which are behind and reaching forward to those things which are ahead, I press toward the goal for the prize of the upward call of God in Christ Jesus.

For the next six days, pay attention to where your focus is drawn. If you notice you're spending more time shopping online, worrying about something you can't control or stuck in any mindless routine, meditate on this verse and pray it over your life. Ask God to help redirect your attention to Him and to help you press toward the goal of living for and serving Jesus.

Divine Instructions

Peace I leave with you, My peace I give to you; not as the world gives do I give to you. Let not your heart be troubled, neither let it be afraid.

John 14:27

Mark 6 gives us a record of Jesus as He finished teaching the multitudes on the shore. He asked the disciples to get in a boat and go over to the other side. In transit from where they were to where they were going, they found themselves in the crosshairs of a massive storm. There they were, toiling and straining, then rowing with all their might as waves pummeled their boat and driving rain pelted their skin.

The last place the disciples, or any of us, wanted to be was in the middle of a storm. After all, just minutes prior to Jesus' instruction to get into the boat and cross the lake, He had performed the miracle of multiplying the five loaves and two fish to feed five thousand people. They watched as this initially meager amount of food fed the entire crowd, and with leftovers to spare!

The King James Version says He "constrained" them to go to the other side (see Mark 6:45). That's a strong word. Jesus did not give them a choice. Notice they were not in the storm because they had messed up. Nor were they there by coincidence or because they were pressured into it by one of their peers. Jesus made them do it. In other words, they were there by divine instruction.

Not long after they obeyed the voice of Jesus, the rain began to fall. Sound familiar? The storm was now raging and the lightning was flashing. They were out some three miles into the water and didn't have a motor or quick access out. They were struggling with what little they had—a set of wooden oars—when it began to dawn on them, "We could lose our lives!"

John 10:10 says, "The thief comes only to steal and kill and destroy" (NIV). This is spiritual warfare. We are in a real battle for our souls, for our families, for our victories . . . for everything! When you became born-again, you not only became an enemy of the kingdom of darkness, but the devil doesn't play fair. Still, rest assured that even in a storm, you are exactly where God wants you to be.

Storms don't come to just whip us into oblivion. When God allows you to go through a severe storm and come out on the other side, you gain a perspective the people sitting on the seashore will never see. You gain an appreciation, a faith, an understanding or revelation, and even an intimacy that you cannot have without going through the trial. You are going to see something only God can show you.

Just don't stop rowing until you get to the other side.

PRAY

Lord, thank You that even in the darkest hour, when the winds roar and the waves roll, You are still with me. I know that the situation I am in does not surprise You. And even if I feel I have no idea what I'm doing, or how I'm going to get to the other side, You have it all under control. Thank You for holding me in the palm of Your hand. In Jesus' name, I pray. Amen.

REFLECT

Recall a moment a storm tested your faith. Name three things you learned from that experience.

ACT

What is the present storm you are in? Do a search of the issue at the core of your storm on a Bible search website or app. Read through the verses or passages that your search pulls up, then pray and ask the Lord to show you which one of those verses applies best to your situation. Memorize it. Now, every time you are tempted to feel discouraged in or about your storm, repeat your verse of hope and promise from God's heart to yours.

Jesus Is Always There

I will never leave you nor forsake you.

Hebrews 13:5

When I first went to Israel and stood before the famous Sea of Galilee, I thought the bus had come to the wrong place. It was not a sea as I had imagined it would be, like the Atlantic or Pacific Ocean, with an endless view of water and no land in sight. At thirteen miles long and eight miles wide, the Sea of Galilee looked more like a large lake. Perhaps it is called a sea because of the three-to-four-foot waves that are created by the sudden storms that sometimes strike the water. The tempests arrive when the cooler air masses from the surrounding mountains collide with the warm air above the lake. Fierce winds can also blow in from the eastern Golan Heights.

The same storm the disciples found themselve in from yesterday's devotion is also recorded in Matthew 14. In this text, it says that Jesus went up to the mountain by Himself to pray (see verse 23). It was hours later, around 3:00 a.m., that Jesus came to them by way of walking on the water.

I wonder how alone the disciples must have felt while they were in the boat and Jesus was up in the mountains. Alone, abandoned, scared . . . surely, they must have felt uncertain. *Where is Jesus? Why would He send us out here? Why didn't He come with us?*

We have similar questions when the doctor gives us bad news or the responsibilities of caring for our children and our elderly parents exhaust our energy and our resources. I want to encourage you today by reminding you that when you can't see God, He can still see you. He notices people who keep rowing in the storm. He sees those who are battered by the waves. Our inability to see Him does not stop His ability to watch us. He sees how hard you are trying. He sees all. You can rest assured that when you're down to nothing, God is up to something.

For when you're battling uncertainty during life's storms, I want to give you three things you can know:

1. **God works.** Even though you can't see Him, He's busy behind the scenes. He hasn't checked out or moved on. He's ceaseless, tireless, and He never stops working. "But Jesus answered them, 'My Father is working until now, and I am working'" (John 5:17 ESV).

2. **God works for the good of those who love Him.** Not for our comfort, pleasure or entertainment, but for our ultimate good. Then again, because He is *the*

ultimate good, would you expect anything less? "And we know that all things work together for good to those who love God, to those who are the called according to His purpose" (Romans 8:28).

3. **God is with you, always.** "I am with you always, even to the end of the age" (Matthew 28:20).

Even though the storms of life can seem, and sometimes truly are, unpredictable, overwhelming and challenging, it is possible to see where God exists in them and possible to feel peace while in them. Reminding ourselves of these three truths adjusts our vision and gives way to finding His peace in the midst of the storm.

PRAY

Heavenly Father, Your presence is such an incredible gift. Thank You that You are with me always, in every circumstance, no matter how I feel or what I go through. I pray my life is lived abiding continually in Your presence. Refresh my spirit when I am weak. Revive me when I stumble. May I never take Your faithfulness for granted. In Jesus' name, I pray. Amen.

REFLECT

Think about a time in your life you felt God was silent when you needed Him. Looking back, how can you see His faithfulness?

— ACT —

Always remember to welcome Jesus on board. He is close to you. A miracle is within your grasp. Grab the oars of faith and take a moment to declare victory in your storm right now. Speak faith over your situation and over all those affected by this or any storm.

Step Out of the Boat

For we walk by faith, not by sight.

2 Corinthians 5:7

When the Bible tells us to "walk by faith and not by sight," notice it doesn't tell us to stay still. It doesn't tell us to wait until we're ready, until we have a strategy perfectly planned out, the right directions to where we are going, or, of course, the exact destination. First, it tells us to walk. To take action. Then, it's a faith thing. Likely, we're never going to "feel" ready because faith isn't about feelings.

When Jesus came to the disciples after they had been battling the winds, waves and rain all night, the men saw what looked like a ghost walking on the water. It was Jesus. They probably thought they were hallucinating. They'd been awake all night long—being tossed about like children's toys—but Jesus quickly calmed their fears, "Be of good cheer! It is I; do not be afraid" (Matthew 14:27).

At the sight of Jesus, Peter grew bold. He asked Jesus to command him to come and walk on the violent seas. Jesus told Peter to come, and the disciple edged out of the teetering vessel. I imagine shock swept over the drenched man as the churning waves roiled over his feet, the rain coming in sideways. A few steps ahead, the fierce breath of the wind almost robbed him of his balance. Fear struck his heart, and Peter began to sink.

Immediately, Jesus caught him and said, "O you of little faith, why did you doubt?" (verse 31). We're quick to point the finger at Peter for his lack of faith, but Peter was the only disciple who took action. Peter was the one who launched out in faith that day when he and the other disciples were on that boat and Jesus came toward them, walking on the water. Eleven other men were there, too, but only Peter took advantage of the opportunity and stepped out of the boat. The others were too scared to so much as talk, even after Jesus told them who He was and instructed them not to be afraid.

Granted, within a few minutes of starting his walk on the water, Peter began to sink. The same thing often happens to us when we step out in faith. It isn't always a bad thing, as it teaches us to truly depend on God, one step at a time. Regardless of the times we sink, I'd rather be a wet water-walker than a dry boat-talker!

Take note—when Peter took his focus off Jesus and started to slip, Jesus stretched out His hand and grabbed hold of him. What Peter could not do on his own, Jesus took over and handled Himself. This should give you confidence as an overcomer to step out of the boat and start walking!

— PRAY —

God, You have not created me to live in a state of fear but in a spirit of faith. With You by my side, there is no need for me to be afraid of anyone or anything. Strengthen my faith when my belief falters and remind me that with You all things are possible. In Jesus' name, I pray. Amen.

— REFLECT —

How do you mature as a Christian from abiding by your feelings to being obedient in faith?

— ACT —

Is there something God has been prompting you to do, but you've been too afraid to step out of the boat and walk? Spend time in honest prayer about this one thing. Be honest and tell God exactly what is holding you back. Then, ask Him for the courage to get out of the boat. Note, most times you won't "feel" courageous, but, remember, having courage looks like just one step of obedience.

A Daily Walking Tip

Come to Me, all you who labor and are heavy laden, and I will give you rest. Take My yoke upon you and learn from Me, for I am gentle and lowly in heart, and you will find rest for your souls. For My yoke is easy and My burden is light.

Matthew 11:28–30

In 1973, an American travel writer named Peter Jenkins set out from Alfred, New York, to walk across America with his dog Cooper. Eventually, his journey ended in Florence, Oregon. His unique journey was chronicled in two books named *A Walk Across America* and *The Walk West*. In the span of those six years, he finds new friends, rekindles his faith, gets married, mourns the loss of his dog who got hit by a car, works odd jobs to make money to continue trekking across the country, and walks in mild and treacherous climates, from blizzards to searing heat. I've heard it said that a reporter once asked him what one thing made him want to quit. It wasn't bad weather, trekking up treacherous mountains or getting mugged, but something on a surprisingly smaller scale—sand in his shoes.

Tiny grains of sand. Little, pesky things. I think about our walk with Jesus and what hinders us in the long walk of faith. It's usually the daily things that tend to pile up when we're not careful. Like spending less time with God. Prioritizing social events or social media or a night of TV binging over studying the Word. Having a packed calendar of everything but the kitchen sink—and matters of the Kingdom. It's the little things that cause worry that eventually accumulate into overwhelming anxiety. Daily temptations. All these things can grind away at our feet so our walk gets shorter, and shorter, and shorter . . . until we can barely remember the last time we were alone with God.

In 2 Corinthians 11, Paul talks about how he was beaten, shipwrecked, robbed, in danger many times, hungry and thirsty, then he says, "besides the other things, what comes upon me daily: my deep concern for all the churches" (verse 28). The daily pressure of all the things can build up to the point where we become too weary to keep walking.

So, what do we do? Bring our burdens to Jesus and let Him carry them. Do you remember at the Last Supper when Jesus washed the feet of the disciples? He wants to do the same to you today. He wants to wash the grainy sands of fear, depression, worry and anxiety off your feet so you can walk daily without giving up.

Will you let Him today?

— PRAY —

God, it's so easy to get distracted by a busy schedule, to get weighed down by responsibilities and carried away by the brevity of my days, and life itself, that I lose sight of my first love . . . of You. Forgive me when I compromise my daily walk with You. Help me to be aware of Your presence every day and of just how much I need You daily. In Jesus' name, I pray. Amen.

— REFLECT —

Whether or not and how often we spend time with Jesus reveals to us if we are prioritizing Him. From the evidence of this in your life, where is Jesus on your list of priorities?

— ACT —

Name two things that you are prioritizing above Jesus. What are two practical steps you can take to lift Jesus above those things? Share this list with a friend and ask him or her to hold you accountable.

Remember the Breadcrumbs

Remember the former things of old,
For I am God, and there is no other;
I am God, and there is none like Me.

Isaiah 46:9

Do you remember what happened prior to the disciples being in the storm on the Sea of Galilee? Jesus fed five thousand people with five loaves and two fish. And there were plenty of leftovers. I bet the disciples took some of the leftovers on the boat with them. Most likely, they'd been out at sea for a few hours before Jesus came to rescue them. At that point, I imagine the leftover food, particularly the fish, would have started to stink. Or maybe the disciples would have already eaten all of the food so that their fingers, greasy from handling their meal, also stunk. Either way, the disciples had some sort of reminder of the miracle they had witnessed hours earlier. Not that they noticed anyway.

When the disciples saw Jesus approaching them, looking like a ghost on the water, they were terrified. "But immediately He spoke with them and said to them, 'Take courage; it is I, do not be afraid.' Then He got into the boat with them, and the wind stopped; and they were utterly astonished, *for they had not gained any insight from the incident of the loaves*, but their hearts were hardened" (Mark 6:50–52 NASB, emphasis mine).

Why were the leftovers so important? Jesus wanted them to serve as a reminder to the disciples in their present danger of what He did for them in the last challenge they faced. He wanted them to know that He is not just God of the shore, but He is God of the sea and God of the storm. The disciples had no reason to doubt Jesus.

Sometimes we have to remind our present of our past. Sometimes we need to reach down, pick up the breadcrumbs and smell our fingers. We have to remember that God is the same yesterday, today and forever (see Hebrews 13:8). He was faithful then. He is faithful now. And He will be faithful tomorrow.

If you're going to survive and overcome the storms of life, you must constantly remember where God brought you from. When I think about where I was to where God has brought me to today, I feel greater faith that He will handle every need in my life. In fact, nobody knows your story like you.

If you're in the middle of a storm now and can't see straight because of it, remind yourself of how God has proven faithful in the past. Remember how God healed you, how He provided, how He opened (or closed) a door, how He saved you, how He delivered you, how He brought you through that hard time, how He connected you with others. Today, Jesus whispers in your ears, encouraging you not to make the same mistake the disciples did. Learn the lesson of the leftovers. Reach back and remember what He has done for you. And remind yourself that He will not fail you now, or ever.

PRAY

God, even though in my heart I believe You are who You say You are, sometimes the difficulties of this life overwhelm me. That feeling causes me to be tempted to doubt, and sometimes forget, what You've already proven to me as truth. Lord, help me to see what You see, and give me more grace when it's most difficult for me to see. In Jesus' name, I pray. Amen.

REFLECT

Spend a few minutes thinking of the last time God worked a miracle on your behalf. What impossible thing came to pass? How did He protect or provide for you?

ACT

Picking up the breadcrumbs helps to position our minds in an attitude of gratitude. There's something about offering God thanksgiving that is powerful. If you take a good look at your life, if you really want to, you might find one hundred reasons why you should cry right now. Or you can do the reverse and find ten thousand reasons why you can smile. It's up to you to decide which perspective you're going to focus on. Write a list of twenty things you are grateful to God for. Be specific.

You're Getting Close

You are of God, little children, and have overcome them, because He who is in you is greater than he who is in the world.

1 John 4:4

While some storms are sent to discourage you and make you want to give up, other storms come because you have attracted the attention of the forces of evil. Many times, these kinds of storms come only when you are close to a breakthrough. It's in times like these that you need to know who you are and Whose you are.

You are more than your credit limit, your zip code, what you did or did not do. As a believer, you are part of a royal priesthood. You are the head and not the tail; you are above and not beneath. You are an overcomer.

Another storm, other than the one I've talked about, is recorded in Mark 5:35–41. I believe the storm that Jesus—who was on the boat with His disciples this time—endured was not a natural storm, but a demonic one. As He approached the area the demonic forces occupied, He knew He was entering enemy territory. The demons immediately recognized who Jesus was, and His mere presence caused such a violent reaction in the spirit world that a storm began to break out even before He arrived on shore. This was a holy area occupied by something unclean.

When you enter or get near a territory the enemy occupies—which could be anything from your school, office, or a neighbor you are witnessing to—that is territory the enemy thinks belongs to him. Your mere presence, and the presence you carry (the Holy Spirit), can create a storm, fierce opposition. Rejoice because you are closer to your breakthrough than ever.

A storm usually is an indication that something big is about to happen.

When Jesus and the disciples got out of the storm and stepped onto land, they encountered the demoniac who was possessed by so many evil spirits that he was cutting himself (see Mark 5:1–20). Jesus cast the demons out of that man, and instantly the demon-possessed man was delivered!

The goal of the enemy is to get your eyes off Jesus and onto the storm. It's because he knows something great awaits you on the other side. It could be a miracle, it could be sobriety, it could be a restored relationship, it could be your loved one coming to Jesus. Whatever it is, something big is going to take place on the other side of the storm. The good news is this: the greater the opposition, the clearer the indication that God is about to set something loose.

Your reward is on the other side of the storm. It is not at the beginning of the trial or in the middle of the struggle when you get discouraged. Your reward is at the end.

Somewhere between sickness and healing, there's going to be a storm. Somewhere between poverty and provision, the storms will come. You may lose your job. Your car may break down. That's okay. It's all part of the victory process when you enter enemy territory.

The storm tells you that you're getting close. The stronger the storm, the closer you are to the point of deliverance. Keep looking to Jesus.

— PRAY —

Thank You, Lord, that Your will is to deliver and set free those who are in bondage. I thank You that the same power that raised Jesus Christ from the dead is the same power that is in me. Remind me of what is on the other side of the storm so I can hold on a little stronger. I know You will give me what I need and complete the work in me that You have started. In Jesus' name, I pray. Amen.

— REFLECT —

Think about the last storm you experienced. Describe your life before, during and after. What did you learn from the experience? Or, if you are in one now, what are you learning in this process?

— ACT —

Memorize today's verse of the day: "You are of God, little children, and have overcome them, because He who is in you is greater than he who is in the world" (1 John 4:4). Post this verse in places where you will see it regularly—on your bathroom mirror, your coffee maker, the fridge, your phone or your calendar. Remind yourself of Who is in you, and Who is here to help you get to the other side.

LOOK AHEAD

The Bible promises in Matthew 24:13 that the one who "endures to the end shall be saved." For many years now, I've enjoyed running. It has a two-fold purpose for me—it's a stress reliever, but most importantly it's also an opportunity to spend time in prayer.

I've learned an important secret about preparing for a successful run. Before I start, I decide exactly how far I'm going to run. If I don't take that first important step, my body will quickly decide that the run is over and almost refuse to take additional steps.

In the same way, making up your mind beforehand to endure the race of faith is the only way to know that you can push through until the end. In Step 3, I'll help you build up your endurance to help you press through and avoid giving up on staying the course for Jesus.

Create the Right Atmosphere

But the fruit of the Spirit is love, joy, peace, longsuffering, kindness, goodness, faithfulness, gentleness, self-control. Against such there is no law.

Galatians 5:22–23

Scripture tells us that spiritual battles take place all around us because we live in two simultaneous atmospheres. One is a physical atmosphere that we can see, smell, hear, touch and taste. The other is a spiritual atmosphere that we cannot see with our natural eye or experience with the rest of our natural senses, but is still very real. The devil knows the power of atmosphere, and as believers, we need to know it as well.

Our attitudes, thoughts and values affect our atmospheres, creating a climate that will then create a culture. If the enemy can get you in his culture using attitudes, thoughts and values that don't align with God's Word, he knows he can get you to sin.

God understands the power of atmosphere as well. He is everywhere—but He does not manifest His presence equally everywhere. He will manifest His presence when the atmosphere is right. He loves an atmosphere of praise and true worship from His people. In fact, the Bible says God inhabits the praises of His people (see Psalm 22:3). When you fill the atmosphere with complaining, faultfinding and murmuring, it's not inviting to the presence of God.

The same is true with the Holy Spirit: atmosphere is everything. The atmosphere of holiness, purity, praise, worship, prayer, love and unity attracts the Holy Spirit; just as an atmosphere of lust, drunkenness, anger and hatred attracts demonic spirits. If you are filled with the Holy Spirit and He is dominating your life, then the fruit of the Spirit—love, joy, peace, longsuffering, kindness, goodness, faithfulness, self-control and gentleness—will become increasingly evident in your life (Galatians 5:22–23). When the fruit of the Spirit is in your life, an atmosphere is naturally created for the presence of the Holy Spirit.

I have heard it said that Christians are not to be spiritual thermometers but spiritual thermostats. In other words, we are not merely supposed to detect the spiritual climate as a thermometer detects the existing temperature in a room; we are to change the spiritual climate, imposing the authority of the kingdom of God wherever we go! It is important to understand atmospheres and our ability to change them because Jesus has authorized and empowered us in this arena.

Jesus changed the atmosphere in His region, and we have the power to change the atmosphere and usher in the presence and power of God in our situations, in our homes and in our churches. This is how we keep the devil out—by imposing the authority of the kingdom of God on him. Keep a spirit of prayer and praise in your life, and it will create the right atmosphere around you.

— PRAY —

Lord, I'm ready to start impacting those around me. Give me the strength and courage to start influencing the atmosphere at work and in my home through Your Holy Spirit. Help me to bring peace and not pain, calm and not chaos. In Jesus' name, I pray. Amen.

— REFLECT —

Are you a thermometer or a thermostat? How can you start changing the climate of your life so it reflects the kingdom of God?

— ACT —

Emotions are powerful. A person's feeling of fear can change the atmosphere of a room. It can almost seem contagious. For the next twenty-four hours, notice what emotion seems to rule you. Are you constantly anxious? Are you often afraid?

What seems to set off your panic easily? Become mindful of what you are allowing to control the atmosphere around you. Pray and ask God for help in that area. Read a book or listen to a podcast about that particular emotion and how overwhelming it is to gain further insight. Talk to a trusted professional for more exploration. And remember, you can't control the atmosphere of every situation, but you can always control your own.

Right Energy Source

For we do not wrestle against flesh and blood, but against principalities, against powers, against the rulers of the darkness of this age, against spiritual hosts of wickedness in the heavenly places.

Ephesians 6:12

I'll never forget what growing up in a Spirit-filled home was like. Every once in a while, when my mother was cooking up a storm, I'd hear a loud sound break out. It wasn't the sound of serving platters or the mixing bowls she was using as she fried up chicken, cooked collard greens and creamed potatoes. My mama would start singing a certain song, and suddenly, she would begin speaking in tongues, the language of the Holy Spirit. It may have been a tad unusual for a child to hear, but it was powerful.

The Bible tells us that in this world, we do not fight against flesh and blood. We fight against powers of darkness. Since we wage war with the supernatural, we must fight with a supernatural source of power. That power is the power of the Holy Spirit.

Satan is after one thing. Like a python whose goal is to suffocate the breath out of its victim, the enemy is trying to extract the breath of the Holy Spirit and His anointing from our lives. Just as a python hates the breath in his prey and will do anything he can to eliminate it, Satan desires to squeeze the Holy Spirit's life out of our churches and out of our personal lives. He wants the breath of life that only comes through the presence and power of the Holy Spirit. Without the power and anointing of the Holy Spirit, we cannot do anything with lasting effect. His Word tells us that it's not by might nor by power, but by His Spirit (see Zechariah 4:6).

When you accepted Jesus Christ as your Lord and Savior, the Bible says that your very heart became the temple of the Holy Spirit. This means, quite simply, that the Holy Spirit lives inside *you*. In short, this is the indwelling Christ, and He will speak to your heart as you go through the highs and lows of this life.

When Jesus gave the Holy Spirit at Pentecost (see Acts 2), He gave us power to do what most would consider impossible. As I stood in the city of Jerusalem during one of my visits, I was reminded of the Upper Room where God sent the Holy Spirit. On that day, we were all given power—power over the enemy, power to move mountains, power that heals, power that produces the anointing that breaks the yoke of sin. God is still in the miracle-working business. Through the Holy Spirit, we have His power living in us to change lives and circumstances in a moment.

If you feel overwhelmed, stuck or defeated, plug into the right energy source today—the Holy Spirit.

PRAY

Lord, sanctify me. I need You. Nothing else will satisfy me. Fill me with the Holy Spirit today. I want to be baptized in the Spirit. I want to walk in the Spirit. I want to talk in the Spirit. I want to live in the Spirit. I don't want to be like everybody else. I'm coming up higher after You. I'm going to seek You with all of my heart. In Jesus' name, I pray. Amen.

REFLECT

What does the power of the Holy Spirit mean to you?

ACT

According to Mark 6, it's possible for God to pass by and His power to not benefit us if we don't make room for His presence. Early in the book of Genesis, it says that the Spirit of God moved upon the face of the waters (see Genesis 1:2).

Notice that the Spirit of God is in motion. The Holy Spirit is always moving. He's not a stagnant pool, not a pond, not even a swamp. In the Scriptures, the Holy Spirit is likened to a river. This means that the power, the provision and the promises of God are passing by, and you and I are supposed to connect with that river. You will receive exactly what your faith reaches out for. Don't let it pass you by. How are you hindering the Spirit of God from moving in your life with His power? How can you resist the hinderances and instead allow Him to jump-start your faith? You can make it happen!

Receive the Right Information

> Your words were found, and I ate them,
> And Your word was to me the joy and rejoicing
>   of my heart.
>
> Jeremiah 15:16

Have you ever felt so bogged down by the cares of this world and the pressure of trying to live your best life that you go numb? The feeling can become so familiar that you easily resign yourself to sitting on the sidelines of your life. You experience no real joy; you just try to get by.

Here's an encouraging truth: It's possible to be anointed and still be weak. In fact, in this life, you will experience seasons where you feel fragile. Still, this truth doesn't change the authority you have in Christ in *every* situation.

Weakness and divine anointing can coexist.

King David knew this coexistence all too well. In fact, this man wrote most of the book of Psalms, a work of beautiful poetry using language that may not always be optimistic, but is real and raw. If he felt alone, he said so. If he felt downcast, he was honest about it.

I find it interesting that the Kingdom of God is one of opposites. It is possible to be poor yet rich, to have joy in the midst of sorrow and peace in the middle of a storm. In 2 Corinthians 12:10, Paul said, "When I am weak, then I am strong." On the surface, that certainly doesn't make sense! Yet, his point was that when we're overwhelmed by the circumstances of this world and feel like we can't handle it anymore, God has more room to work in our lives. This is true, of course, when we allow the right information to sink in.

I think about Gideon hiding in a cave at a time when the nation needed a great leader. The Bible says that the angel came and said, "You are a mighty man of valor." And Gideon replied, "But I am the youngest from the smallest tribe, and I'm poor. I don't have anything. Are you hearing me, God? I'm the least of my brothers," (see Judges 6:11–15). In other words, get someone else to do the job! In essence, Gideon was saying, "I'm not the one, this is not the place, and now is not the time." But God saw it differently. What I love about Gideon is that, even after his vehement protest, when God finally and emphatically made it clear that he was the one He'd chosen, Gideon's response was surrender. "I am the one, this is the place, now is the time." (see Judges 6:17).

Gideon made the shift from reluctance to surrender because he allowed the right information to sink in. He wasn't restricted by the limitations of his low self-esteem; he chose to believe what God said about him.

What you take in determines what you will see. If you receive bad or frightening information, you'll see a world of fear and hopelessness. God doesn't just declare what we are today, He declares what we will be tomorrow through His strength. When you continually feed yourself a diet of God's Word, you'll be able to endure anything!

— PRAY —

Lord, sometimes I set a low standard for myself. Instead of standing on Your promises and believing what You say about me, I cower in fear or insecurity because I don't feel like I am enough. Remind me that You have called me, that I am wonderfully and fearfully made, that You have a plan and purpose for my life—and that it is good! In Jesus' name, I pray. Amen.

— REFLECT —

What is your heart like when it comes to receiving the Word of God? How agreeable are you to what the Bible says about you?

— ACT —

Read James 1:23–24: "For if anyone is a hearer of the word and not a doer, he is like a man observing his natural face in a mirror; for he observes himself, goes away, and immediately forgets what kind of man he was."

What are some areas of your life in which you are not aligned with what God says in His Word? Write them down. Maybe you don't believe you'll conquer that addiction, nor do you believe that you are more than a conqueror as the Bible declares (see Romans 8:37). How will you begin to delete that faulty thinking and start downloading the right information?

Right Location

"Fear not, for I am with you;
Be not dismayed, for I am your God.
I will strengthen you,
Yes, I will help you,
I will uphold you with My righteous right hand."

Isaiah 41:10

During a time of famine, God gave Elijah a clear instruction saying, in effect, "Go to Cherith. I have commanded the ravens to feed you there" (see 1 Kings 17:4). God told Elijah that if he moved to the right place, supernatural provision would also show up.

Sometimes, enduring the race of faith means discerning the place of blessing for your life. If God says, "I'll bless you 'there,'" and you insist on staying "here," then you're going to miss His provision. Everything was dependent upon Elisha being in the right location.

The right location doesn't have to do with a physical location only. Just about the time Elijah thought he had God

89

all figured out, the brook suddenly dried up, and the ravens stopped bringing food. I once preached a sermon called, "What to Do When the Brook Goes Dry and the Birds Won't Fly!" In it, I explained that the only reason God lets the brook dry up is because He wants to drive you back to your source. We are to seek God's face, not His hand. We want a handout, but God wants a face-off.

Don't fall in love with the method and forget that God is your source. The brook wasn't Elijah's source; God was. We get married to a method, but we must be open to change. When the Holy Spirit wants to do a new thing, we have to get away from the old wineskins. In this case, God gave Elijah a new plan, "Go to Zarephath. . . . I have commanded a widow there to provide for you" (1 Kings 17:9).

Many times, we trust in systems instead of trusting in God, but God is our source. When Elijah met his protégé, Elisha, Elisha was plowing in the field. Elijah knew Elisha was the next prophet in line, so he threw his mantle on him. In those days, this was a custom that represented being chosen to follow in one's footsteps. Elisha was blown away in gratitude, but before he took off with Elijah, he made one request: "Let me say goodbye to my parents first, and then I'll follow you" (see 1 Kings 19:20). Elisha returned to his fields. Then, to outsiders looking in, it looked like he caused some property damage. He killed his livestock, burned his equipment, and he served the meat to the people. Now, he was ready to follow Elijah.

This was not a violent act; it was an act of significance. The plow represented the security in Elisha's old life. His livestock and equipment were his livelihood. The plow also represented acceptance in the community's economy of farmers, of which Elisha was a part. Before he could step into the destiny God had created for him, he had to break the plow.

If God says, "I'll bless you 'there' or 'this way,'" and you insist on staying "here" or doing things "that way," then you'll miss His blessing and provision. Trust God and follow Him and stay planted in the right location.

— PRAY —

Father in heaven, I'm ready to break the plow and be open to a new location. Instead of trusting in my comfort, my preferences and the old ways of doing things, I trust in You with all my heart. Help me to no longer lean on my own understanding and instead acknowledge You in all my ways. Direct my path. Help me get rid of old plows and show me new ways. In Jesus' name, I pray. Amen.

— REFLECT —

When is the last time God moved in a new location (way) in your life? What was the outcome?

— ACT —

We hold tenaciously to old plows that have served their purpose at a different time because it can be scary to let them go! What old plow are you clinging to right now? What is so hard for you to let go of? Spend some time in thought and prayer for why that might be. Ask God to release your grip and to help your feet take one step forward in the direction of a new location.

Surround Yourself with the Right People

Faithful are the wounds of a friend,
But the kisses of an enemy are deceitful.

Proverbs 27:6

Looking ahead is impossible in isolation. Relationships matter. It's important to link hands and hearts with others who will deposit faith in your spirit.

When God chooses to bless you, he sends a person. When Satan chooses to discourage you, he sends a person. Some people can help advance your purpose, and there are some sent to snuff it out. We must be spiritually discerning. When times get tough, we persevere by choosing the right people to have alongside us.

When people step into your life, they don't just bring their bodies—they bring their spirits. There are two kinds of people: "flesh people" and "faith people." Flesh people tear you down and feed your fears, while faith people build you up and feed your faith.

Flesh people waste your time and drain your energy. Faith people are the kind who inadvertently fill your life. They draw you closer to being the person God created you to be. They are the ones who will be lovingly honest with you. They are strong when you are weak.

The early Church rejected Paul because he had persecuted Christians before his conversion. The disciples were afraid of him so God sent a person: Barnabas. Barnabas used his influence with the disciples to get Paul's foot in the door of the church. Barnabas was the right person in Paul's life.

In life, you've got to have the right people surrounding you. The right people are those who encourage you, who love you and who will be honest with you. They don't tell you only what you want to hear; they tell you what you're supposed to hear and what you need to hear.

Some of you don't have God's blessing because you aren't doing life with the right people. You are surrounded by people who are negative, who don't put God first, who care more about material things than spiritual matters. If you're struggling in a particular area, don't be around somebody who is struggling with the same thing. You need to be around a person who is strong in the area in which you are weak. You need to spend time with somebody who knows how to go where you are trying to get to.

If you have spent your life gravitating toward all the wrong people, I have good news for you. God will bring the right people to your life and toss out the wrong people. But when He makes the exchange, don't return to the wrong people. "Every branch in Me that does not bear fruit He takes away; and every branch that bears fruit He prunes, that it may bear more fruit" (John 15:2). That does not mean the wrong people are inferior and you're superior; it just means they are not a part of God's plan for your life.

Keep looking, praying and seeking until you find the right people . . . those who draw you closer to being the person God purposed you to be.

PRAY

Dear God, thank You for creating us to be in relationship with You and with other people. I ask that You help me be a better friend to others. Help me to love better, show more grace and serve others well. Give me discernment and wisdom in choosing the right people to walk alongside in this journey of faith. In Jesus' name, I pray. Amen.

REFLECT

Proverbs 11:14 says, "Where there is no counsel, the people fall; but in the multitude of counselors there is safety." Who are the godly people in your life whom you respect and ask for feedback when you need to make an important decision?

ACT

Devote the next seven days to praying for meaningful relationships. Ask God to send the right people into your life. Also, commit to being the right kind of friend to those God brings into your life.

Maintain the Right Focus

Do not withhold good from those to whom it is
   due,
When it is in the power of your hand to do so.

Proverbs 3:27

Another way to build up your endurance and push through resistance is to dial in your focus. Job knew this secret. This man lost his health, his wealth and his children in a single day. Amid these tragic losses, he never lost his faith. How was that possible? He had the right focus.

I find Job 42:10 fascinating. It reads, "And the Lord restored Job's losses when he prayed for his friends. Indeed the Lord gave Job twice as much as he had before." Notice *when* God restored Job's losses: It was *when* he prayed for his friends. In his hurt, his pain, his tears, his bad days, the mornings he didn't want to get out of bed, the prayers that left his lips unanswered, Job focused on others. And in the moment he did that, God turned his world around and blessed him in the trial.

In 1 Kings 17, Elijah paid a visit to a widow who had just enough flour left in her barrel and just enough oil in her jug to make one last, small cake for herself and her son. The drought had become so pervasive that people were starving. She intended for that small cake to be the last meal she and her son would ever have.

But then Elijah showed up in her life. And of all things, the prophet asked her to make him a cake to eat first. Here we have a woman with a seed and a man with a need. The widowed woman was forced to decide. *Do we eat this food and die, or do we shift our focus and take care of others even though we have needs in our own lives?* The moment she got the right focus, put all she had left into the hands of the prophet and obeyed God, something supernatural happened. "The bin of flour was not used up, nor did the jar of oil run dry, according to the word of the LORD which He spoke by Elijah" (1 Kings 17:16). Because the widow had chosen the right focus, every day for three and half years, she and her son had enough to eat.

We all have needs. And God knows what each of them is. He also knows what happens when we decide to shift our focus off of ourselves and focus on someone else. Remember, what you keep in your own hand shrinks, but what you put in God's hand multiplies.

In the early 1900s, General William Booth, the founder of the Salvation Army, sent a telegram to encourage his officers around the world. Telegrams were expensive, charged by the word, so Booth had to come up with something powerful yet short. He managed to sum it up perfectly in one word: others.[1]

Others became the focus of the organization of the Salvation Army, and it still is today. May the same ring true for our lives.

— PRAY —

Dear God, it's so easy to stay trapped in my own world, thinking only of myself, my needs, what I'm missing, what I've lost and what I want. And yet, You've called me to stretch and reach beyond myself. Help to turn my focus away from myself and onto others. Use me to be someone else's miracle. In Jesus' name, I pray. Amen.

— REFLECT —

When has someone else sown into your life, even while they had needs of their own? How did it impact you?

— ACT —

Identify someone that you know who needs your help. Maybe it's a neighbor who just had surgery and could use a few meals or housekeeping. Maybe you know a single mom who could use a hand with childcare. Maybe your local food pantry is running low, and though you're living on a limited income, your garden has a surplus. This week, do something for someone no matter how down and out you feel. God sees!

Get in Sync with the Right Timing

My times are in Your hand.

Psalm 31:15

Keeping time in the United States during the late 1800s was complicated. There was no single standard. For the most part, people kept time by looking at the position of the sun. This was before the invention of mechanical clocks. Most big cities had a clock in the center of town that everyone could see. The problem was, the time was off between cities. Sometimes by a few minutes, sometimes by far more.

Railways operated independently and on their own time-tables. Like railways, cities each ran on a different time. This caused much confusion and led to dangerous conditions. Imagine the logistical nightmare of making travel plans or coordinating cargo deliveries—or, even worse, safety issues like two trains barreling toward each other from different directions because their schedules did not line up.

Finally, the heads of the major railroads collaborated to solve the problem. On November 18, 1883, they established the Standard Time system, which divided the United States and Canada into five time zones.[2] On that day, at exactly noon on the 90th meridian, workers at every railroad station reset their watches and clocks to reflect the new Standard Time within their designated time zone. While a win for the railways, not everyone was happy. Many people decided to stick with whatever time they had established through whatever means. In some places, the gap between local time and Standard Time was as long as 45 minutes![3] Some cities even refused to switch to the new time. Arguments erupted . . . towns were split . . . until another solution, a permanent one this time, was established 35 years later when Standard Time was enacted by legislation for the entire United States. Everyone had to fall in line with the new standard.

The right timing is important. Ecclesiastes 3:1 declares that there is "a time for every purpose under heaven." Purpose is connected to timing. God's promises always have a time frame on them.

The right time to serve the Lord is always now. The right time to be committed to Him is always now. The right time to do His will is always now. Are there certain requests you are praying to God for and wondering why they're not being answered? I don't know the reason for it, but I know God knows the right timing. He wants you to get in sync with His clock.

I love how Psalm 37:34 reads in The Living Bible: "Don't be impatient for the Lord to act! Keep traveling steadily along his pathway and in due season he will honor you with every blessing." Bad times don't last forever. The key to continuing to stand is to get in sync with God's clock for your life.

— PRAY —

Father in heaven, forgive me for my impatience as I have tried to hurry Your plan and purpose for my life and taken matters into my own hands. Those plans have always failed. I trust You to answer my prayers in the right timing. Help me to wait as long as necessary. In Jesus' name, I pray. Amen.

— REFLECT —

Think of a time when you decided not to wait for God's timing and took matters into your own hands. What was the end result? What did you learn?

— ACT —

What is the thing that you're waiting on the Lord to do right now? Choose to trust that because He loves you ardently, His timing and His answer will be delivered at just the right moment and in just the right way. Trust that the end result will be both for His greatest glory and your greatest good.

The Right Mind

Therefore, preparing your minds for action, and being sober-minded, set your hope fully on the grace that will be brought to you at the revelation of Jesus Christ.

1 Peter 1:13 ESV

The mind is a battlefield, one in which the enemy is trying to capture yours and win. The good news is that we are not left defenseless against the ploys of Satan. He may wage war with us, but through Jesus, we win! I want to show you just how important the mind is as you strive to be an overcomer.

In ancient times, leprosy was a disease that affected the skin, causing severe skin sores and nerve damage. It was thought to be a curse of the gods or punishment from sin. In Leviticus 13, the Israelites were given different signs to look for if they showed symptoms of the disease. The chapter continues with an in-depth description of the examination process the priest would have to conduct if someone presented themselves with such a skin condition. I'd read this before, but never noticed the significance of verses 42–44 until recently:

And if there is on the bald head or bald forehead a reddish-white sore, it is leprosy breaking out on his bald head or his bald forehead. Then the priest shall examine it; and indeed if the swelling of the sore is reddish-white on his bald head or on his bald forehead, as the appearance of leprosy on the skin of the body, he is a leprous man. He is unclean. The priest shall surely pronounce him unclean; his sore is on his head.

Notice that verse 44 says, "The priest shall surely pronounce him unclean." This is not your standard unclean. A footnote in my Bible in the NKJV mentions unclean as "altogether defiled." Other translations say "utterly unclean." Now, prior to this verse, the word "unclean" is mentioned fifteen times and the word "plague," twenty-seven times. But everything shifts in verse 44 as "unclean" and "plague" become worse. Why? Because the leprosy has gone to the head!

The disease of leprosy represents the battle of our minds. If the enemy has your mind, he has you! If there ever was a time that we needed to protect our minds, our thought life, the purity of our minds—it is now.

Paul gave us powerful instructions on how to battle the enemy in Ephesians 6. He told us to "take up the whole armor of God, that you may be able to withstand in the evil day, and having done all, to stand" (Ephesians 6:13). One of the tools we have in this spiritual arsenal is the helmet of salvation.

It would be crazy to ride a motorcycle without protecting your head. The same is true for a Christian. It would be crazy to let your mind think whatever it wants; therefore, we need to control our thought life. In the same way, the helmet of salvation is for protection. We must take the necessary spiritual measures to protect our precious gift of a mind.

If you know who you are and Who it is that has called you, you will be able to endure anything.

— PRAY —

Lord, I know full well that my mind is a battlefield. I have lost battles more times than I can count. I thank You that through Your sacrifice I can transform. I am a new creation in Christ. Remind me to replace my old thinking for new thinking, and my old ways for new ways. Enable me to renew my mind in Your Word each day. In Jesus' name, I pray. Amen.

— REFLECT —

If the enemy gets into your thinking, he will contaminate your mind, your beliefs and your faith. What happens when your thought life becomes "tainted" by the enemy?

— ACT —

Read and memorize Philippians 4:8:

Finally, brethren, whatever things are true, whatever things are noble, whatever things are just, whatever things are pure, whatever things are lovely, whatever things are of good report, if there is any virtue and if there is anything praiseworthy—meditate on these things.

The Word of God is another weapon in our spiritual arsenal. Remind yourself of this verse when your mind starts thinking thoughts that are negative, self-defeating or not God-honoring. Then replace those thoughts with truths from God's Word that are true, noble, just, pure and lovely.

LOOK OUT

Satan wants nothing more than for you to stop caring about a lost and dying world. Yet, this is one of the most important visions God wants you to have during these overwhelming times. When the disciples were asking Jesus for a sign of the end times, He told them "This gospel of the kingdom will be preached in all the world as a witness to all the nations, and then the end will come" (Matthew 24:14).

In other words, spread the Good News! Tell someone about Jesus. Yes, life is overwhelming, and the stresses we experience weigh us down, but at the same time, the harvest is plentiful. Don't miss the opportunity to share the hope of the Gospel any chance you get!

It's Your Job

How then will they call on him in whom they have not believed? And how are they to believe in him of whom they
have never heard? And how are they to hear without someone preaching?

Romans 10:14 ESV

When you think of an evangelist, who comes to mind?
You might picture a preacher standing on a platform.
Or maybe you envision someone holding a sign that says,
"Jesus is Coming Soon!" on a busy city sidewalk. Perhaps
you're imagining the people who knock on doors and profess
their faith to strangers with pamphlets and a Bible in hand.
However, what about you? Have you ever considered yourself
an evangelist? If not, consider this:

> Deliver those who are drawn toward death,
> And hold back those stumbling to the slaughter.
> If you say, "Surely we did not know this,"
> Does not He who weighs the hearts consider it?

He who keeps your soul, does He not know it?
And will He not render to each man according to
his deeds?

Proverbs 24:11–12

The responsibility of evangelism is entrusted to every believer. You included. The Scripture above tells us to "deliver those who are drawn toward death, and hold back those stumbling to the slaughter." Those are strong words. We are not to be believers who sit on the sidelines watching as others go to hell without hearing the message of salvation. We have a responsibility to share the Gospel.

This startling reality ought to move us. It ought to stir us. It ought to bring us to our knees. It ought to burden us. Christianity is not about getting every prayer answered and living a perfect life; it's about loving, serving and sharing with others the message of hope that has changed us.

God wants to use you. He put people in your life that only you can reach, that only you can carry a burden for, that only you and your testimony can break through their darkness.

There are unbelievers who may never hear the truth of Jesus Christ if you do not bring it to them. When you share the hope of Christ, invite someone to church or tell them about your faith, you're planting a life-giving seed in a moment that cannot be relived. God has placed you in that path for such a time as this and entrusted you with His hope, His Word and His story. You'll never know what lies on the other side of your obedience without being obedient to this

God-entrusted responsibility. Where would you be today if someone had not shared His story with you?

We say we "follow" Jesus, but if we are not compelled to share His love, it is time to reevaluate what we truly believe. It is not your responsibility to force someone into a relationship; that's the job of the Holy Spirit. It is your job to plant seeds, even if they don't appear fruitful. Obedience to share Christ's love, death and resurrection is all God requires of us. God will do the rest.

— PRAY —

Dear God, the most important gift You gave me is the death and resurrection of Your Son, Jesus Christ. Forgive me for the times I have been too scared or embarrassed to step out and share hope with others. I will not be ashamed to be a witness. I will not be ashamed of the gospel of Jesus Christ, for it is the power of God unto salvation. So, Lord, I'll share my story. I'll pray and intercede for my lost family members and friends. In Jesus' name, I pray. Amen.

— REFLECT —

Are you sitting on the sidelines, or are you sharing Jesus with others?

— ACT —

It may feel a bit out of your comfort zone, but this week, ask the Lord to reveal to you who needs to encounter His love. You might very well have unbelievers in your direct circle of influence. Start there. Choose someone to share the Good News with this week (and don't stop!).

Before You Go . . .

I will give you a new heart and put a new spirit within you;
I will take the heart of stone out of your flesh and give you
a heart of flesh.

Ezekiel 36:26

Before Jesus gave the disciples the Great Commission as recorded in Mark 16:15 to "go into all the world and preach the gospel to every creature," He expressed some disappointment. All this took place after His death and resurrection. The Bible tells us:

Later He appeared to the eleven as they sat at the table; and
He rebuked their unbelief and hardness of heart, because they
did not believe those who had seen Him after He had risen.

Mark 16:14

Jesus was getting ready to tell His disciples to go into all the world and preach this Gospel, but before He could do it, He needed to do something. He had to get rid of two things inside of them: their unbelief and their hardness of heart. This speaks to us today. Before we can share Jesus with others, we need to look inside of ourselves and examine our hearts.

Do you suffer from unbelief? Has your heart grown cold? Has your love for God waned? Have you stopped believing that God can soften even the hardest of hearts and bring them back home to Him?

I'm reminded of what Ecclesiastes 11:1–2 tells us:

> Cast your bread upon the waters,
> for you will find it after many days.
> Give a serving to seven, and also to eight,
> For you do not know what evil will be on the earth.

Casting your bread upon the waters is a reference to your testimony. Jesus calls Himself the Bread of Life. The job of the Christian is to cast the bread. What this Scripture is telling us to do is to cast the bread out without giving up. In other words, cast out our testimony without getting a hard heart, without worrying about getting rejected, without doubting the outcome, without being pushy or arrogant. Just keep sharing the Good News of Christ. And what next? After many days, it will come back. This is why we are not to give up on our spouse, our neighbor, our coworker, our social media friends or the strangers we meet day in and day out.

We don't know when the hour of salvation is for anyone; it's not in our power to know nor is it to save them—that's God's job! Our job is to share and to share in faith.

Some of us need God to deliver us from hardened hearts and a disbelief that the Gospel message doesn't work, that it's boring or old-fashioned or not relevant anymore. If you are going to successfully preach Jesus to people, do some soul-searching. Does your heart need a revival today? Ask God to revive your spirit and refresh your soul. Remind yourself why the Good News is called good. Remember where you came from and where you are today. Fall in love with Jesus all over again. When you have that newfound zeal, it's going to be hard not to talk about Him.

— PRAY —

So I say, Lord, restore my compassion. Restore my tears. Restore my vision for the lost. None are hopeless. None are helpless. Jesus has not given the responsibility for the selection of His bride to any one of us. He chooses whom He will. Renew in me a zeal to carry the Gospel to people near and far. In Jesus' name, I pray. Amen.

— REFLECT —

In what situations has your heart grown cold?

— ACT —

Is there someone in your life that you have doubted God could save? I want you to spend the next twenty-one days in faithful prayer for this person's salvation. Come to God, in faith, with this person's name, then believe that with Him all things are possible.

Be a Nighttime Hero

Let your light so shine before men, that they may see your good works and glorify your Father in heaven.

Matthew 5:16

The greatest story for Christians is the story of the resurrection. Still, prior to the resurrection, there was an event that holds an incredible lesson for believers today. In this story, an unusual hero named Joseph of Arimathea emerged and used his influence for good in a time of darkness.

Now when evening had come, there came a rich man from Arimathea, named Joseph, who himself had also become a disciple of Jesus. This man went to Pilate and asked for the body of Jesus. Then Pilate commanded the body to be given to him. When Joseph had taken the body, he wrapped it in a clean linen cloth, and laid it in his new tomb which he had hewn out of the rock; and he rolled a large stone against the door of the tomb, and departed. And Mary Magdalene was there, and the other Mary, sitting opposite the tomb.

Matthew 27:57–61

Two things immediately stand out to me in this passage of Scripture. First, Joseph of Arimathea was a rich man who was also a disciple of Christ. Jesus Himself said, ". . . it is easier for a camel to go through the eye of a needle than for a rich man to enter the kingdom of God" (Matthew 19:24). But Joseph was different. He understood that his riches and influence were to be used for God's purposes.

Joseph of Arimathea used his position and power to provide a place for the body of Christ. As a member of the prestigious Sanhedrin Court, Joseph was a respected member of the community. He used his position to gain an audience with Pilate. Only a man of wealth and respect could get the attention of the ruler.

The second lesson that jumps out at me is that Joseph of Arimathea had a mission—to provide a resting place for the body of Christ in his city. And he was intent on accomplishing that purpose . . . even if he had to beg for it.

Scripture literally says Joseph "begged" for the body of Christ. He had a passion for it. Our Lord's body was torn, twisted, tortured and bloody, but Joseph didn't care how bad it looked. He didn't care how torn and ripped the precious body of Christ was. He begged for Christ's body anyway.

I think this is a beautiful analogy for the Body of Christ today. We must use all of our influence and power to beg to provide a place for the Body of Christ today. If you look around, you'll see people who are torn apart, bloody and battered spiritually. We must have compassion for the lost.

Joseph of Arimathea used his success as a businessman and a respected member of the community to provide a place for the Body of Christ. That commitment impacted one of the very foundations of our faith—the Resurrection story. Are you using your influence to make plans for the Body of Christ in your community?

— PRAY —

Lord, help me to stop being a consumer and start being a giver. Reveal what I can offer on Your behalf to bring hope to a hurting world. Give me opportunities to be a hero for You in the nighttime hour. In Jesus' name, I pray. Amen.

— REFLECT —

What is keeping you from being a nighttime hero?

— ACT —

Pray and ask the Lord to use your hands, your heart and your resources, and to make you a hero in the night. What unique influence or platform do you have to help reach the lost, the hurting and the broken? Use that as your starting point.

Don't Abandon the Church

On this rock I will build My church, and the gates of Hades shall not prevail against it.

Matthew 16:18

The Church is under attack today. While church attendance has been dropping steadily in the past decade, it took a deeper hit during the COVID pandemic and has yet to recover.[1] Attendance by older adults (65+) and young adults (18–34) dropped by about 10 percent between 2019 and 2021.[2] More than 1 in 4 pre-COVID churchgoers are still missing on Sunday mornings, according to Lifeway Research. It's an improvement from early 2021, but still not at the 91 percent who said they plan to return.[3]

In some ways, the state of the Church today is in its night hour. However, it's also beautifully positioned for heroes, like Joseph of Arimathea, whom you read about in yesterday's devotional.

Joseph begged for the body when the deity had departed. At the time, it was just a physical body in its most vulnerable position. It had no power in it. It had no miracles in it. It had no victory. It was not extremely joyful or excited. Still, that was the moment when the hero in the night stood up and begged to get involved.

Anybody can get involved in a church when the pastor is going viral for something cool, when it's packed out, when miracles are happening, when it's having a mountaintop season. But how many of us honor, defend or fight for the Church when there is nothing it can do for us? Like when attendance is down, when money is tight, when the programs aren't flashy or there aren't enough bright lights or loud music. At the moment when Joseph stood up for the body of Jesus, it was in a time of transition. And Joseph refused to be a traitor in transition.

God wants to transform us from consumers to givers. Many could have been present when Jesus died. They all could have asked for and cared for the dead body of Christ, but only one man did. There was no benefit to Joseph in doing so, but he did it anyway because of the love he held in his heart for Jesus. When the body of Christ was dead and most vulnerable, God used one willing person to take care of that body.

It isn't time to leave the local church when it's going through hard times and everyone else has bolted. That's when it's time to double down on your commitment. That's when you can become a hero in the night. Remember what Jesus told Simon when He changed his name to Peter, "And on this rock I will build My church, and the gates of Hades shall not prevail against it" (Matthew 16:18).

There will be a comeback! You want to be a part of it. Be a hero when others are not even showing up. The Church is coming back in a bigger and more powerful way than ever, and He is presently looking for the people who will lead that movement. Why not you?

⸺ PRAY ⸺

God, forgive me for the times my commitment to the local church was solid only because I benefited in some way. I want to be a light and of service to the Body of Christ. I want to stay planted and grow even when it looks dry or barren. Show me the areas in which I can serve and the opportunities in which I can make a difference for You. In Jesus' name, I pray. Amen.

⸺ REFLECT ⸺

Why does the local church matter?

⸺ ACT ⸺

Has your church attendance waned over the last few weeks, months or even years? Perhaps you've been committed to attending weekly services regularly but haven't been involved in serving others. Consider your commitment level to your local church and, starting this week, up your game. Invest more of you into the Body of Christ.

Start at Home

Train up a child in the way he should go,
And when he is old he will not depart from it.

Proverbs 22:6

Sometimes, looking *out* means taking a closer look *inside* of our homes. We should be influencing the ones we live with, or the ones who know us the most, for good. I recently asked a Hispanic friend of mine if his children speak Spanish. "No," he replied. "I wish they did. But to be honest, my wife and I don't speak Spanish around the house. We are just so busy that even though it's the language we were raised with, and we are bilingual, our children never hear us use it in the car or in our home." His answer struck me as an illustration of our spiritual voices.

Our children must hear us declaring our faith, speaking our prayers and our praise and demonstrating our relationship with Jesus. If the words we use in our homes don't model a Christian lifestyle, our children will never become fluent in it themselves. Living as Christians must be done daily. And this doesn't just apply to our words, but to our lifestyle as a whole.

There's an interesting story in the book of Nehemiah that explains what I'm talking about. Nehemiah discovered that his native language was dying in the city of Jerusalem. The people had broken their covenant with God, and as a result, the city was nearly destroyed. Only a small remnant remained when Nehemiah arrived to start rebuilding the Temple. He heard Hebrew children playing in the streets and noticed they weren't speaking Hebrew (see 13:23–24). As we continue to read, we see that Nehemiah was enraged by this discovery because the loss of their language would mean the people of God would lose their culture. This very thing is happening in Christian homes today.

The twenty-first-century church is marrying the spirit of this age and raising a generation of children who do not know the language of God. They don't know the language of praise and prayer that pulls down strongholds. This generation has adopted the language of the culture.

It's not enough to speak the language of God in church once a week. It must be spoken fluently at home if you expect your children to learn and speak it, too. In other words, model what you preach. Lead by example. How is your language? What tone of voice do you use with your family and others? Do you listen to your kids? How is your behavior when you are angered? How do you speak with and treat your spouse? How do you handle conflict? Our actions and our words leave lasting impressions.

God has a purpose for our kids and for the next generation. We raise them with one goal in mind: that they will someday make the right decisions without us alongside to make those decisions for them. Never forget that though the times and people change, God does not change. Help them put down roots of faith that will stand the test of time and launch them to new heights.

— PRAY —

Father in heaven, You have entrusted my children to me. What a privilege! Guide my words and my actions so I do the right thing and show them what integrity and good character look like, especially when it's not easy. Give me the strength to stand firm and the wisdom to make good decisions for my family. Help me to lead them well. In Jesus' name, I pray. Amen.

— REFLECT —

What role do you play in your child's life? If you don't have children, do you have regular interaction with a younger sibling, a niece or nephew, or a friend's child? What influence do you have on him or her?

— ACT —

Here are three practical ways to look out from the home front, right where you are now. Let these guide your priorities.

1. Make sure your private life matches your public life.
2. Teach your children to honor God and His house.
3. Center your family on God's purposes.

Reach Beyond the Walls

Let each of you look out not only for his own interests, but also for the interests of others.

Philippians 2:4

When Jacob was old and on his deathbed, he pronounced prophetic blessings on each of his sons. His next-to-youngest son was Joseph. In Genesis 49:22–24, we read the words Jacob spoke over him:

> Joseph is a fruitful bough, a fruitful bough by a well; his branches run over the wall. The archers have bitterly grieved him, shot at him and hated him, but his bow remained in strength and the arms of his hands were made strong by the hands of the Mighty God of Jacob.

The picture Jacob paints of Joseph's life is that of a bountiful, thriving, walled-in garden planted next to a well. The garden is so lush that branches grow over the wall and reach out into neighboring areas. Jacob mentions the hatred and mistreatment Joseph encountered, but accurately highlights Joseph's ability to stay faithful to God through any trial.

In the verses that follow, Joseph is given a mighty blessing from his father. Jacob promises a greater blessing to Joseph than to any of his brothers. Jacob says that because Joseph extended his reach beyond the walls, God will increase Joseph's blessing.

When famine struck Egypt and the surrounding areas, Joseph had provided for his brothers, who had sold him into slavery. He provided for Potiphar's wife, who falsely accused him. He provided for Potiphar who threw him in jail even though he was innocent.

All these people would have died in the famine if not for Joseph. Instead, Joseph extended his blessing beyond the walls, beyond his confinement, beyond where he was. He cared about people who had nothing to offer him, people who didn't deserve his help. He shared his blessing with people around him. See, Joseph didn't keep the blessing of his garden inside the walls. Instead, he reached out to meet the needs of others.

The well mentioned in this passage of Scripture represents Jesus Christ—the Living Water. When we find the Living Water, He changes our lives. Jesus turns our lives around and makes us new. He generously showers us with abundant blessing.

The question is, are we sharing what we have with those beyond these walls? Beyond these walls are people who are lost and don't know that Jesus can rescue them. Beyond these walls are the hopeless, defeated, afraid and bound.

We have the Living Water, but we must send a vine beyond the walls. We can't come to church week after week, experience the saving power of Jesus, live in His blessing and keep all of it to ourselves. Don't keep Jesus to yourself—reach out beyond these walls!

— PRAY —

Lord, give me Your eyes to see beyond the walls, Your heart to desire to reach out past those walls and Your grace to follow through that which is Your calling to us all, as believers. In Jesus' name, I pray. Amen.

— REFLECT —

The joy of living for Jesus is not just going to church. It's when we get so full of the Living Water that we can't help but share our joy with others. What keeps you from sharing the love of Jesus with others?

— ACT —

One of the greatest ways we can share Christ is by sharing our story with others. Have you ever shared with someone else your testimony of how Jesus saved you? It's powerful. It's your story, unique to you. Spend time writing down what your life was like before meeting Jesus, how you came to be saved and what has changed as a result. Keep it simple. This will come in handy next time you reach beyond the walls of the Church and pass along the Living Water.

Be a Burden Bearer

Bear one another's burdens, and so fulfill the law of Christ.

Galatians 6:2

There is only one place in Scripture, Matthew 21:1–3, where we are told that Jesus had a need:

Now when they drew near Jerusalem, and came to Bethphage, at the Mount of Olives, then Jesus sent two disciples, saying to them, "Go into the village opposite you, and immediately you will find a donkey tied, and a colt with her. Loose them and bring them to Me. And if anyone says anything to you, you shall say, 'The Lord has need of them,' and immediately he will send them."

We come to this place in the New Testament during which Jesus is entering into the last week of His physical life here on Earth. He says, "I need a donkey. Actually, I need that one. And if anyone tries to stop you, tell them the Lord needs that animal." Note that Jesus didn't say He needed a white stallion or a powerful Clydesdale. Jesus chose a donkey.

God uses lowly things. He uses burden bearers. He uses people who get up under a load that is so heavy that, at times, though they feel like they can't keep going, they just keep bearing the load. I want to give you six key lessons Jesus teaches us from this illustration that will help you look ahead:

1. **The greatest blessings come from the greatest burdens you bear**. You cannot have the blessings without bearing the burden.

2. **Jesus calls the unqualified**. If you feel unimportant, unqualified and inadequate, you are in the company of some of the most notable people in the Bible, including a shepherd boy, a prostitute, a fisherman and a tax collector.

3. **Jesus will do the heavy lifting**. All Jesus asked to do with the donkey is to let Him ride it. He promises to do the rest. Matthew 11:28–30 tells us, "Come to Me, all you who labor and are heavy laden, and I will give you rest. Take My yoke upon you and learn from Me, for I am gentle and lowly in heart, and you will find rest for your souls. For My yoke is easy and My burden is light."

4. **A donkey is built for endurance, not speed**. If God is going to use you, His intention for you isn't for you to make a quick sprint then go missing six months

later. The kind of people that God chooses and uses are the ones who will choose to endure through the times when the load gets heavy.

5. **You carry the burden, but be sure God gets the glory**. There's a difference between confidence and arrogance. You had better give God the glory if He's blessed you.

6. **Jesus can't use you until you've been untied**. As long as you're tied to the post, the scenery never changes. If you allow Jesus to untie you, to loose you and lead you, He will take you to a place where the scenery changes.

God isn't looking for stallions; He's looking for burden bearers like you.

— PRAY —

Father in heaven, I am so grateful that You chose the ordinary things and the people of this world to make an extraordinary difference. Thank You for using me. Thank You for the opportunity You give for me to be a burden bearer for You. I want to do what You have called me to do, and to do so in Your strength. Open my eyes and my heart to the things I am tied down to that are keeping me from moving forward. In Jesus' name, I pray. Amen.

— REFLECT —

What weight are you still carrying that you need to surrender and let Jesus carry for you?

— ACT —

Name the one relationship or dysfunction in your life that you are tied to that is keeping your scenery the same. What three steps do you have to take to untie yourself from that unhealthy connection?

Be Excellent

Then this Daniel distinguished himself above the governors and satraps, because an excellent spirit was in him; and the king gave thought to setting him over the whole realm.

Daniel 6:3

In the Bible, Daniel was captured as a teenager and brought to the idol-worshipping kingdom of Babylon. His integrity, meticulous attention to his work and dedicated spiritual life all distinguished him from those around him and brought glory to God. These even earned him a significant promotion within the Babylonian kingdom. Even though his peers were determined to destroy him by finding fault in his life, they found nothing to use against him.

The world responds to excellence. When someone has been successful and lives a life of integrity, we turn our ear to what they have to say. From businessmen to athletes, performers to educators, craftsmen to healthcare professionals; when you're excellent at what you do, people want to know your secret. And people will listen to what you have to say.

As Christians, we are called to be influencers for Jesus, inside and outside of our families, homes and communities. Recently, I saw a guy standing on the side of the street holding a sign that read, "Jesus is returning September 22." Now, there's nothing wrong with street evangelism. Sharing the Gospel is the goal, right? That said, I wouldn't suggest putting a date on the return of Jesus. Now think about this: How much influence does a stranger on a street corner holding a sign announcing Scripture to all have on the average person? Frankly, not much.

People are looking for proof. They are looking for hope in real life, in everyday living. When God sent His one and only Son, He was spotless—without blemish. If God sent us His best, it is only appropriate that we present back to Him our best. Whatever He has placed in your hands, pursue it with excellence! When you do so, doors you could never have imagined will open, and you will gain favor with people and influence for the Kingdom!

I love what Jesus said in Matthew 5:14–15:

> You are the light of the world. A city that is set on a hill cannot be hidden. Nor do they light a lamp and put it under a basket, but on a lampstand, and it gives light to all who are in the house.

You are the light! Wherever you are, God has placed you on a lampstand. How brightly you shine will be your choice. You can hide under a bad attitude, sloppy work, questionable character or negativity; or you can do whatever you are tasked with in the everyday with excellence and make people wonder what's different about you.

We represent God's kingdom here on earth. It's time to examine our lives. We must do our very best for Jesus because the world is watching us. We must not settle for mediocrity and sloppy living. We are anointed to rise above an ordinary, common life and live with a spirit of excellence.

PRAY

Lord, I know that I am a reflection of You. Unfortunately, I often fail in being a good example. Still, I want to strive for excellence. I want to do the best at whatever it is You put in front of me. Remind me to focus on what matters most. In Jesus' name, I pray. Amen.

REFLECT

Why do we sometimes settle for mediocrity rather than strive for excellence?

ACT

Do you find yourself lacking in excellence in many important areas of your life? It's possible you're trying to do too much! Being busy has become a value in American society, even a badge of honor for some. Take time and prioritize what's most important to you. Focus on four to five key areas that matter the most. Then start doing your best and excelling in those areas, rather than trying to do everything at once—and doing a mediocre job at best.

LOOK UP

Not only should we look out for others as the end approaches; we must also look up.

Luke writes in his gospel, "Now when these things begin to happen, look up and lift up your heads, because your redemption draws near" (Luke 21:28).

Our posture as believers is one of great hope and great promise. We can look up because God made us promises and will not abandon our families until redemption, or grace, draws near to our house. Not only do we have the power of salvation as a reason to look up, we also have the power of Jesus Christ in our spirits. I've written this final set of devotions to give you reasons to not give up and instead look up in overwhelming times.

God Sets the Pattern

He has made everything beautiful in its time.

Ecclesiastes 3:11

God never changes. He is the same yesterday, today and forever (see Hebrews 13:8). The Bible says that the things that were written before time were written for our learning. The Word of God shows us the pattern of God. If you want to understand the way God is moving today, go back and look at the patterns in the Scripture. Let's look at Genesis 15:13–14. God is prophesying to Abram:

> Know certainly that your descendants will be strangers in a land that is not theirs, and will serve them, and they will afflict them four hundred years. And also the nation whom they serve I will judge; afterward they shall come out with great possessions.

There's a pattern here. God is giving Abram a heads-up that his descendants will end up in bondage serving another nation. And while they will stay in that place for four hundred years, at the end of that time period, they are going to be free and come out with great possessions. Abram's descendants wouldn't leave Egyptian bondage the same way they went in. God had a plan, and the plan was on a time schedule.

This speaks to us today. God puts a limit on trouble. If there is a beginning, there will always be an end.

We are reminded in the book of Job that God will set an end to darkness. Job went through unimaginable loss. There was a beginning to it and an end. And what did God do afterward? He blessed Job with double what he had before.

Daniel is another example. God told this man that the people of Israel would be taken into captivity by Babylon and serve under King Nebuchadnezzar. But after seventy years, the nation would be free and come home where they belonged. There was a beginning and an end.

There is so much darkness in this world that it's easy to think the government, the economy, a health crisis or our township's board of education has all the control; that it's up to them to set the limits on when we are going to come out of the darkness and into the light. But that's not the case. All we must do is look at the pattern God gives us in the Bible. He has the power. He sets the limits. He knows the timeline. Our job is to trust Him and be ready.

In John 2:19 Jesus said, "Destroy this temple, and in three days I will raise it up." He wasn't talking about Herod's temple, the actual building, but the death and resurrection of His physical body. He was saying, "I'm going to be crucified. It's going to get rough. It's going to look bad. It's going to look like I've been defeated. But in three days, I'm going to defeat death and rise again." This is the pattern!

Don't worry about the expiration date for your trials; know that the Lord has already set the end date.

— PRAY —

Father in heaven, thank You for being a light onto my path. The dark consumes me at times. It's a place I can't hear You or see You or feel You. I don't like it, and I need Your strength to get through it. May I hold tight to the promises in Your Word rather than to my feelings or to the opinions of others. And may my faith get stronger during these times knowing there is an end date to my trouble. In Jesus' name, I pray. Amen.

— REFLECT —

How does knowing that God sets an end to darkness fill you with hope?

— ACT —

Think of two people you know who are going through dark times. Call or text them today and pray for them. Ask God to fill their hearts with peace and hope as they trust in Him during their trials.

Show Yourself Alive

But God, who is rich in mercy, because of His great love with which He loved us, even when we were dead in trespasses, made us alive together with Christ.

Ephesians 2:4–5

In Acts 1:3, Luke writes how Jesus "also presented Himself alive after His suffering by many infallible proofs, being seen by them during forty days and speaking of the things pertaining to the kingdom of God."

After he suffered, Jesus showed Himself alive. This is an important principle for us to remember as we endure and look up in trying times.

Think of it this way. Jesus went through trouble on earth prior to His experience on the cross. He was mocked. Many didn't believe who He really was. He was betrayed by those closest to Him. Calvary was a different experience. The wounds ran much deeper. Calvary scarred Him. Calvary marred Him. Calvary changed everything! And while He was hanging on the cross, right before He breathed His last breath, Jesus cried, "Father, 'into Your hands I commit My spirit'" (Luke 23:46).

Some trials will change your life. When a trial marks you, you must put your spirit into the hands of God. Don't allow the most difficult trials to make you bitter. Give them to the Lord, and He will turn them into testimonies. Jesus knew the only safe place He could put His spirit was in the hands of His heavenly Father. It was only in His hands that He could become Life again.

We know, of course, the crucifixion isn't the end of the story. I love how another translation says that Jesus showed Himself alive. He didn't just show up. He showed Himself alive. That He conquered death. That He did what He said He would do. That He was still standing! And just like you learned yesterday, that's the pattern!

Most of us have been hit hard the past few years. Some of us have endured multiple hits. It's time to show ourselves alive! It's the wrong time for a pity party, for us to wallow in despair, for us to throw in the towel and quit. It's the right time to talk life, to preach hope to ourselves and to a dying world and to come alive again!

You may have gone through the fire, but you're still standing. You may have been thrown into a lion's den, but you're still reading these words. Some things may have scarred you permanently, but never forget that you are a chosen vessel and a royal priesthood.

Fix your eyes on the prize. There is a great day coming. The difficult times we are in are simply tremors for the return of Jesus!

Just as Jesus showed Himself alive "after His suffering," there is an "after this" for you. After your test, after your struggle, after your addiction, after your loss, after your miscarriage, after your bankruptcy, after the shattered dream, after the broken heart.

You are still God's man or woman, and His plans for you cannot be thwarted.

Decide today that you are victorious, regardless of the circumstances. You are alive and you are still here. Show yourself alive, and allow the Lord to shine on a dark world through you.

— PRAY —

Dear Jesus, I take this opportunity to thank You for my victory. I am saved, delivered and healed. I am an overcomer! I win because You are my God. I win because I am Yours. I can show myself because You are the Resurrection and the Life. I believe that I will begin to see miracles in my life as I take Your Word and believe Your promises, declaring in the face of the enemy, "It is written." Thank You. In Jesus' name, I pray. Amen.

— REFLECT —

If you are going through a difficult period right now, name two things you are grateful for that give you strength, hope or peace.

— ACT —

Hard times have a way of knocking us out, but they also have the potential of knocking us to our knees. When's the last time you prayed on your knees? Take a few minutes today to talk to God while kneeling (if physically possible). Being in a humbling position often helps to change our perspective.

Overcome with Faith

. . . above all, taking the shield of faith with which you will be able to quench all the fiery darts of the wicked one.

Ephesians 6:16

One of the biggest obstacles to us living the life of an overcomer is fear. Fear is rampant in the world and in our lives. We are afraid of what might happen or what might not happen. We fear outcomes, relationships, failure, people's opinions, the list goes on. Yet, if fear rules our lives, we will not dare to step out in faith to fulfill our destiny in God. The Bible says that without faith it is impossible to please God (see Hebrews 11:6).

You cannot succeed in life if you give in to fear. Here are six steps to help you fight fear with faith and overcome!

1. **Preach to yourself.** When God asks me to do something that seems impossible for me, I have to preach to myself to defeat the fear and uncertainty that try to control me.

2. **Keep trying.** Whether in a relationship, in business, in reaching your personal goals, never give in to fear and quit trying. The important thing to remember when you fail, make a mistake or hit a detour is not to quit.

3. **Don't believe what you see.** Have you been defeated because of what you saw with your eyes? Has the promise of God been aborted because you chose to believe what you saw instead of what God had said in His Word? Don't believe what you see only with what your senses tell you. Walk by faith in God's promises.

4. **Tame your talk.** "Devil talk" will bring the devil on the scene and "God talk" will bring God on the scene. You will always experience attacks from the enemy trying to pull you out of God's presence, out from under His shadow. But confessing the truth of the Word of God will keep you from falling prey to the enemy's tactics.

5. **Take risks.** Fear fighters take advantage of opportunities. They don't wait to be attacked; they go on the offensive when opportunity presents itself. If you sing, join the choir. If you are thinking about starting a new business, take the steps to investigate your possibilities. If you are lonely, make the effort to develop friendships.

6. **Remember God is the Master of Disaster.** When disasters strike, the good news is that God is Master

in times of disaster. Whether from your poor choices or from circumstances beyond your control, when you call on God, He will resolve your situation. Even if your distress is self-inflicted, God has a plan to get you out. You don't need to be tormented by fear.

There is no match for the power of faith released in your life. Faith praises God for the answer before it comes. It steps on the neck of every lie that opposes the purposes of God for your life. Faith can move mountains and always does the will of God in and for you. It's time for you to look up. Keep overcoming with faith!

— PRAY —

Lord Jesus, I thank You that my life changes today. You have not given me a spirit of fear. You have given me a spirit of power, of love and of a sound mind. The blood You shed on the cross frees me from shame and delivers me from my weaknesses. Fill me with good courage. Fill me with a fearless spirit. You are with me. I will not be afraid. In Jesus' name, I pray. Amen.

— REFLECT —

Can you think of a time in your life when you were scared to do something you knew you had to do, but you went through with it anyway? How did you feel afterward?

— ACT —

Search through Scripture and find and meditate on three verses that have to do with fear. You can even start with the Scripture at the top of this devotional if you'd like.

Post one or two in a place that you'll see right when you get up in the morning, maybe on your phone or night table. As soon as you wake up, remind yourself that fear has no power over you.

Courage with Cold Feet

Be on guard. Stand firm in the faith. Be courageous. Be strong.

1 Corinthians 16:13 NLT

Speaking of fear, do you know the story of Benaiah in the Old Testament? He was a hero during the reign of King David and became one of the king's mighty men. The Bible says that he killed a lion in a pit on a snowy day. Imagine that! He had the courage to jump down into a snowy pit with a lion and fight with him to the death. I call that courage with cold feet!

When we say we have cold feet, we mean we are afraid to do something. Courage is doing what you are afraid to do. I've heard it said that "courage is fear that has said its prayers."

When you hear from God and He tells you to do something, you are filled with faith in that moment. It braces your spine like steel. Then, when you actually move out in faith, you encounter the lion that is about to attack. The apostle Peter tells us that we are in warfare with a lion: "Be sober, be vigilant; because your adversary the devil walks about like a roaring lion, seeking whom he may devour" (1 Peter 5:8). That is when you get courage with cold feet. But it's all right. God needs some men and women in these troubled times who have the courage to say, "God said to do it, and I am going to do it!"

The fact is, there is no real courage unless you are scared! You may be at a point in your life right now where God has told you to do a hard thing, but you have started to feel the cold feet syndrome. Forget about looking up, you can't even put one foot in front of another. Let me encourage you: Be of good courage; the Lord is with you! Begin to declare, "Jesus is with me, and He has all power. I have faith for this!"

When you are facing insurmountable odds, you are in the realm of courage with cold feet. I know that place well. When God told me to go to Gainesville, Georgia, to pastor Free Chapel, I went in courage with cold feet. When He said to build a church building, 2.5 million dollars seemed like 29 million dollars. Our congregation moved forward in courage with cold feet. Then when we bought more land for five million dollars, we had to summon courage to conquer our fear again. And when we began to build a sanctuary for seventeen million dollars, I said, "Here I am again, moving forward in courage with cold feet."

I wish every story ended with a miracle or healing, but it doesn't always happen that way. Sometimes God takes you through the fiery-furnace experience instead of delivering you from the fiery furnace. However the story ends, know that God is always with you, and He will use every story for His glory.

So start moving! He doesn't mind your cold feet one bit!

PRAY

Dear Jesus, forgive me for not taking steps in faith because I've thought my cold feet were inadequate. I choose to obey Your commands and to go forward in courage even when I feel afraid. Thank You that even if I walk through the valley of the shadow of death, You are with me. You are my Light and my Salvation. With You by my side, I can do whatever You have put before me. In Jesus' name, I pray. Amen.

REFLECT

What have you been putting off that you know you must step out in faith and do?

— ACT —

Acknowledge the cold feet you feel in relation to your response to the previous question. Ask God to gird you in His strength, and then do that thing. Make the phone call. Take the interview. Say yes. Say no. Move forward with cold feet.

The Praise Strategy

To console those who mourn in Zion,
To give them beauty for ashes,
The oil of joy for mourning,
The garment of praise for the spirit of heaviness;
That they may be called trees of righteousness,
The planting of the LORD, that He may be glorified.

Isaiah 61:3

The Christian life is a battlefield with an enemy whose goal is to try to defeat us every day. But God has given us strategies for winning, and praise is one of them. When Israel's army went into battle, the tribe of Judah led the way. The name "Judah" means praise. Are you overwhelmed by the battles of life? Pull out the weapon of praise and look up.

When praise leads the way, victory is on the way!

This same praise strategy toppled the walls of Jericho for Joshua and caused Jehoshaphat's enemies to destroy one another before the battle even began (see 2 Chronicles 20). King Saul used the same praise strategy when he asked

David to play the harp for him so the king could find relief from the troubling spirits that tormented his soul (see 1 Samuel 16).

In fact, Isaiah 61:3 introduces us to the praise strategy when it speaks of exchanging the spirit of heaviness for the garment of praise. When depression, worry, fear and other negative emotions attack you from all sides, you can't just get rid of them with a snap of your fingers. You must replace them with something else. In this case, you put on the garment of praise.

I think of Paul and Silas sitting in a filthy prison cell with their hands and feet in stocks. They were tired, hungry, and bloody and sore from being beaten. In the midnight hour, they began to pray and sing praises to God. In other words, they looked up! I love what the Bible says happened next.

> Suddenly there was a great earthquake, so that the foundations of the prison were shaken; and immediately all the doors were opened and everyone's chains were loosed.
>
> Acts 16:26

Praise opens doors. Praise unlocks opportunity. Praise confuses and drives the enemy crazy. When you face a situation you can't handle, make the decision to praise God instead of worrying about your problem. You may not feel worthy—but He is! You may not feel able—but He is! You may not feel like you have control over your life—but He does! Remind God of His promises. Nothing moves Him like the sight of His children praising His name and claiming His promises in the face of adversity. Jesus said, "You will have complete and free access to God's kingdom, keys to open any and every door" (Matthew 16:19 MSG).

Praise invites God to intervene, so use it. And while you're at it, find somebody to join you (see Matthew 18:19). Like Paul and Silas did together, multiply your impact before the throne of God.

Start lifting up praise and victory will be on its way!

─ PRAY ─

Lord, teach me to live with a heart of praise. May I be a worshipper in good seasons and bad seasons. You are holy and true, powerful and mighty, worthy of all of my praise. Let not the rocks cry out before I have a chance to worship You. Before I start my day or put my head down to sleep at night, I want to give You praise for all You have done and for Who you are. In Jesus' name, I pray. Amen.

─ REFLECT ─

How has praise changed your perspective and/or attitude?

── **ACT** ──

Memorize Psalm 34:1: "I will bless the LORD at all times; His praise shall continually be in my mouth."

Start a habit of committing at least ten minutes a day to praising God. You can do this on your way to work, while you exercise, during your quiet time or as you get ready for the day.

Get the Picture

Where there is no vision, the people perish.

Proverbs 28:18 KJV

Sometimes in order to look up, you need to get the picture God sees. If I look around the world today, it doesn't look like a very positive image. But we don't have to let what our current situation looks like dictate the image we see. We need to imprint on our vision what God sees for us.

How do you see yourself, your family, your future? If you only see hurt, disappointment and failure, then that is likely the direction you are heading. But what if you get a picture of how God sees you? Over and over in the Bible we see God give His children a picture, a dream, an illustration to help make His promises clear.

In Judges 7, God promised Gideon He would deliver the Midianites and Amalekites into his hands. At first, Gideon wasn't convinced. The three-hundred-man army of Israel was outnumbered, out-resourced and out-planned by the

135,000 soldiers from Midian. So God told Gideon to take his servant and go to the enemy's camp and spy on them.

God knew after Gideon heard what he was going to hear, he would gain strength and confidence (see Judges 7:9–11). When the two men arrived, a soldier was telling a friend about his dream:

> "I have had a dream: To my surprise, a loaf of barley bread tumbled into the camp of Midian; it came to a tent and struck it so that it fell and overturned, and the tent collapsed."
>
> Then his companion answered and said, "This is nothing else but the sword of Gideon the son of Joash, a man of Israel! Into his hand God has delivered Midian and the whole camp."
>
> Judges 7:13–14

Upon hearing this—*boom!*—Gideon got a picture in his mind. He saw God's promise coming to pass. He saw victory. He saw God using him.

A promise from God is a revelation of God's divine intentions in your life through Scripture. The key is to turn the promise into a picture. You will never possess the promises of God until you see them. If you see them, then God can bring them to pass. Before a promise or a prophecy will ever manifest, you must picture it in your mind. If you see it, you can have it. If you see it, God can do it. If you see it, it can become a reality.

Believing something is crucial, but so is seeing it. Without vision, the people perish (see Proverbs 29:18). In other words, if there is no vision for the future, there is no power in the present. The more vision you have for your future, the more power you have for your present.

If your mind is persuaded by a picture, then your body begins to respond. Let a picture form in your mind of God's promise to you, and He will begin to develop it into reality.

— PRAY —

Lord, I need help correcting my vision. All I've been looking at are the facts that surround me, which aren't so encouraging. But Your promises are greater than facts. I pray for vision for my life, for my situation, for where I am and where I'm going. I commit to walking out the vision you give me, as Gideon did. In Jesus' name, I pray. Amen.

— REFLECT —

Have you ever had to look beyond the facts and use your imagination to see the possibilities? How did that help you push through a situation to your goal?

— ACT —

Today I want you to do exactly what the title of this devotion says: get the picture! Human beings prefer visual imagery over words. Imagine listening to a presentation absent of engaging graphics. Boring, right? Now think of something that's been on your heart that aligns with Scripture. Maybe God has promised healing, or restoration of a relationship or freedom over an addiction. Get in your mind the picture of what it looks like to be healed, to have your relationship restored or to live in freedom. Now think about that!

Encourage Yourself

The Lord is my strength and my shield;
My heart trusted in Him, and I am helped;
Therefore my heart greatly rejoices,
And with my song I will praise Him.

Psalm 28:7

First Samuel 30 opens with David and his mighty men coming home after a long journey being away. What greets their eyes crushes their spirits. The village is decimated. Much is burned to the ground, including David's home. The men's families? Gone. The Amalekites had captured them all.

David finds himself in a hard place. The joy of his past military victories fades as he realizes his family is gone. Talk about being discouraged. Ever been there? One minute you're living your best life and the next—*boom!*—an unexpected event throws you a curve ball. It gets worse for David. While he is grieving his losses, his men turn on him. They decide he's the one to blame and that he needs to be stoned. As David is standing before his comrades, distressed in his spirit, he does something unexpected. "David strengthened himself in the LORD his God" (1 Samuel 30:6). Devasted by his circumstances and accused by his friends, David turns to God alone for the encouragement he needs.

There comes a time when we realize we won't get the help or the hope we need from others. In these moments, we must look up by encouraging ourselves in God. Here are three practical ways to do this:

1. **Rehearse your past victories.** I wonder if David did that. In the moment he found himself homeless, his family kidnapped and his soldiers seconds away from stoning him to death, I wonder if he closed his eyes and remembered what it was like being in the valley with Goliath. Maybe he remembered the times that God had spared his life when he was on the run from Saul. Perhaps he remembered what it was like tending sheep one afternoon and the following day being anointed with oil by the prophet Samuel to be the next king of Israel. Close your eyes and count your blessings.

2. **Remember you're under divine protection.** What or who are you battling today? When your resources are depleted and you think you're going under for the last time, God has provided a refuge that's higher than your circumstances, a place where you're under divine protection and the enemy has no jurisdiction. Angels are protecting you. There may be battles ahead, but God's protection is your promise. "When the enemy

comes in like a flood, the Spirit of the LORD will lift up a standard against him" (Isaiah 59:19).

3. **Remind yourself who your God is.** He is able. He is a way maker. He is a miracle worker. He is the very door you need when it seems like all other doors are closed. I didn't know He was more than enough until I didn't have enough. I want you to remind yourself who your God is.

He is your God, and don't you forget it!

— PRAY —

God, victory is mine. Thank You so much that victory is mine. I exercise my faith in You and offer my thanksgiving. It doesn't matter what is happening to me or around me, You are an anchor in my storm. May I be like David, a believer after Your own heart, and learn how to encourage myself instead of relying on external circumstances or others to lift my spirit up. I look up to You, and You alone. In Jesus' name, I pray. Amen.

— REFLECT —

Recall the last time you have witnessed someone encourage themselves immediately after a devastating situation. What impression did that leave on you?

ACT

Read the following names of God. Spend a few minutes meditating on each name. Take to heart which name speaks to you most in this season of your life. Remember, He is that for you.

- God is Jehovah-Jireh, your provider.
- God is Jehovah-Nissi, your victory banner.
- God is Jehovah-Tsidkenu, your righteousness.
- God is Jehovah-Shalom, your peace.
- God is Jehovah-Shammah, the God who is there.
- God is Jehovah-Rapha, the God that heals you.

Heaven Is Waiting

For our light affliction, which is but for a moment, is working for us a far more exceeding and eternal weight of glory,
while we do not look at the things which are seen, but at the
things which are not seen. For the things which are seen are
temporary, but the things which are not seen are eternal.

2 Corinthians 4:17–18

Satan tries to keep us focused on our problems so we forget
about our promises. He wants us to live shallow, earth-
bound lives. Our enemy wants us to focus on the temporary
and lose sight of the eternal, because we become dangerous
to his plans when we have eternity in our sight. He doesn't
want us to remember we are headed for heaven.

We need to have heaven on our mind. This is the ultimate
reason to have a look-up spirit, knowing we will spend eternity with our Lord Jesus Christ.

This world is not our home; we are just pilgrims passing through. When you have been through the heat and the
pressure of life and feel like you have nothing left, I want to

remind you that you have eternal life in heaven with God to look forward to. A kingdom without end where all things will be made new. "And God will wipe away every tear from their eyes; there shall be no more death, nor sorrow, nor crying. There shall be no more pain, for the former things have passed away" (Revelation 21:4).

The Apostle John wrote the following words while marooned on the Isle of Patmos:

> After these things I looked, and behold, a door standing open in heaven. And the first voice which I heard was like a trumpet speaking with me, saying, "Come up here, and I will show you things which must take place after this. Immediately I was in the Spirit; and behold, a throne set in heaven, and One sat on the throne."
>
> Revelation 4:1–2

Alone on the island, God allowed John to see a door. From behind the door, he heard a voice saying, "Come up and see what heaven is like. Are you having a bad day, John? Maybe a bad month? Come up here and look at things from heaven's perspective."

Jesus Himself said in John 14 that heaven was a real place being prepared for all of us to live in. Believe it—heaven is real. This world isn't our final destination. It isn't our true home. Our home is with our Father in heaven.

Do you know why we have a generation who doesn't think purity and holiness matters? It's because they don't really believe Jesus is coming back to take us to heaven.

We're told in 1 John 3:2–3, "Beloved, now we are children of God; and it has not yet been revealed what we shall be, but we know that when He is revealed, we shall be like Him, for we shall see Him as He is. And everyone who has this hope in Him purifies himself, just as He is pure."

When we have heaven on our minds, we want to be pure. We want to be purified and prepared. Whether things are going well or falling apart, come up here.

Look up. Keep heaven on your mind. If you believe in and trust in Jesus, this is where you are headed!

PRAY

I admit, Lord, heaven isn't always on my mind. I quickly forget that the gift of salvation gives me eternity with You in heaven. What a gift! I pray that what I do on earth means more than temporary praise or pleasure. Help me to align my priorities and responsibilities with eternal things, matters of significance. I want to make my life matter for Your return. Help me to live ready. In Jesus' name, I pray. Amen.

REFLECT

Have you ever stopped to consider that Jesus really could come back at any time? If He were to come back tonight, what is left undone? What do you plan to do about that?

— ACT —

While we must keep heaven on our mind, we also can't be so heavenly minded that we become of no earthly value. Write down two ways you can practically look up toward heaven yet engage in what God has called you to do today.

NOTES

Step #1 Look Within

1. "The Power of Positive Thinking," Health, Johns Hopkins Medicine, accessed December 12, 2022, https://www.hopkinsmedicine.org/health/wellness-and-prevention/the-power-of-positive-thinking.

2. Ibid.

3. Bernie Lincicome, "Honesty Not Only Best Policy, It's the Only Policy among Pros," *Chicago Tribune*, August 10, 1989, https://www.chicagotribune.com/news/ct-xpm-1989-08-10-8901040404-story.html.

Step #2 Look to Jesus

1. "It's a Wonderful Life Beginning with Prayers and Angels Talking," YouTube, https://www.youtube.com/watch?v=79pIurpNARs.

2. Tino Wallenda, "The Show Must Go On," *Victorious Living*, May 2019, https://victoriouslivingmagazine.com/2019/04/the-show-must-go-on/.

Setp #3 Look Ahead

1. "Others," About Us, Salvation Army Tuscon, accessed December 13, 2022, https://www.salvationarmytucson.org/about1-ch7r.

2. Randy Alfred, "Nov. 18, 1993: Railroad Time Goes Coast to Coast," Wired, November 18, 2010, https://www.wired.com/2010/11/1118railroad-time-zones/.

3. Fran Capo, *It Happened in New Jersey* (Guilford, Conn.: Globe Pequot Press, 2004), 69.

Step #4 Look Out

1. Wendy Wang, "The Decline in Church Attendance in COVID America," *Institute for Family Studies* (blog), January 20, 2022, https://ifstudies.org/blog/the-decline-in-church-attendance-in-covid-america.

2. Joe Carter, "Don't Blame the Pandemic for Low Church Attendance," The Gospel Coalition, January 29, 2022, https://www.thegospelcoalition.org/article/church-attendance-pandemic/.

3. Aaron Earls, "5 Current Church Attendance Trends You Need to Know," Lifeway Research, February 2, 2022, https://research.lifeway.com/2022/02/02/5-current-church-attendance-trends-you-need-to-know/.

Jentezen Franklin is the senior pastor of Free Chapel, a multi-campus church with a global reach. His messages influence generations through modern-day technology and digital media; his televised broadcast, *Kingdom Connection*; and outreaches that put God's love and compassion into action. Jentezen is also a *New York Times* bestselling author who speaks at conferences worldwide. He and his wife, Cherise, live in Gainesville, Georgia, and have five children and five grandchildren. Find out more at JentezenFranklin.org.